YO-BBY-699

Peter Ralston

The Acts of Individuals

Community, like charity, begins at home. Worried that extortionate real estate prices would force local people off the nearby waterfront, the owners of an island store sell some of their land to young fishermen at a fraction of its market value. Sixty miles to the east on the mainland, a retired woman arranges shared ownership of her wharf with the 24-year-old fisherman who stacks his traps there, ensuring his access to the water after her death. Neither of these transactions is motivated by greed or even by tax deductions; both demonstrate that some people are willing—when the future of their community is at risk—to act on their own.

Communities are as fragile, and as strong, as those who live in them. Differences of opinion will divide the members of a community from time to time; whether they come back together will depend on hard-to-define qualities like leadership, the willingness to forgive, the ability to see things from another's point of view.

The authors and editors responsible for this edition of Island Journal—Volume 19—have considered many aspects of communities, from many different points of view. There is music. There is history. There is shared responsibility for natural resources. There is tragedy. And always, there is possibility: the schoolchildren who learn a new technology so they can better understand their town's natural systems; the city that makes a commitment to preserving its working waterfront.

In a fickle world the life of a community is never certain or guaranteed. But the individual actions of citizens, particularly those who act to make the future better and the community stronger, are evidence that communities can—if we let them—survive and even prosper.

The Editors

ISLAND JOURNAL

The Annual Publication of the Island Institute
Volume Nineteen

Cover: Peter Ralston

**ISLAND
INSTITUTE**
Publishers of Island Journal and Working Waterfront

Sustaining the Islands and Communities of the Gulf of Maine

ISLAND JOURNAL

PUBLISHER
Philip W. Conkling

EDITOR
David D. Platt

ART DIRECTOR
Peter Ralston

COPY EDITOR
Esme McTighe

GRAPHICS RESEARCH
Jessica Baines

DESIGN
Mahan Graphics, Bath, Maine

PRINTING
The J.S. McCarthy Co., Augusta, Maine

●

ISLAND INSTITUTE

PRESIDENT
Philip W. Conkling

OFFICE AND OPERA-
TIONS ASSOCIATE
Kathy Allen

EXECUTIVE
VICE PRESIDENT
Peter Ralston

INFORMATION
SERVICES MANAGER
Richard Davis

VICE PRESIDENT
FOR FINANCE AND
OPERATIONS
Josée L. Shelley

FINANCE MANAGER
Norene Bishop

VICE PRESIDENT
FOR PROGRAMS
Sandra Thomas

RECEPTIONIST/
CUSTOMER SERVICE
ASSISTANT
Allison Philbrook

EDUCATION OFFICER
James Doyle

FINANCE ASSOCIATE
Joann King

COMMUNITY
PLANNING OFFICER
Nathan Michaud

ARCHIPELAGO
MANAGER
Patricia Montana

MARINE RESOURCES
FIELD OFFICER
Corrie Roberts

ARCHIPELAGO
BUYER/MERCHANDIS-
ING ASSISTANT
Bren Grigo

MARINE
RESOURCES OFFICER
Ben Neal

ARCHIPELAGO
SALES CLERK
Katherine Oakes

GIS/WEBSITE
DIRECTOR
Chris Brehme

ISLAND FELLOWS
Candyce Dunham, Keith Eaton,
Allyson Fauver, Mike Felton,
Erin Fisher, Nathan Geraldi,
Emily Graham, Nathan Gray,
Sherry Ann Marcum, Daniel
O'Grady III, Kathleen Reardon

PROGRAMS
COORDINATOR
Leslie Fuller

PROGRAMS ASSOCIATE
Chris Cash

TEMPORARY POOL
Bethany Allen, Emily Allen,
Anne Baldridge, Sharon Bartoo,
Hannah Berger, Kate Griffin,
Marcia Reisman, Karen Rector,
Pat Ritchie, Jessica Stearns,
Sally Thibault, Parker Tootill

PUBLICATIONS
DIRECTOR
David D. Platt

GRAPHIC DESIGN
ASSOCIATE
Charles Oldham

PUBLICATIONS
MARKETING
ASSOCIATE
Mike Herbert

BOARD OF TRUSTEES

CHAIRMAN
Horace A. Hildreth, Jr.

COMMUNICATIONS
DIRECTOR
Linda Cortright

VICE CHAIRMAN
John A. Bird

DEVELOPMENT OFFICE
MANAGER
Jane White Desaulniers

TREASURER
John P.M. Higgins

SECRETARY
Donna Miller Damon

DEVELOPMENT
ASSISTANT
Laurel Ingraham

CLERK
Michael P. Boyd

MEMBERSHIP
COORDINATOR
Jody Herbert

TRUSTEES
Robert P. Bass, Jr.
Louis W. Cabot
Eric Davis
William J. Ginn
Polly Guth
Margery M. Hamlen
David L. Lunt
Eldon C. Mayer, Jr.
Peter Quesada
George T. Shaw
Samuel Parkman Shaw
Barbara Kinney Sweet
David Thomas

MEMBERSHIP
DEVELOPMENT
ASSISTANT
Kathy Estabrook

EXECUTIVE ASSISTANT
Judy Tierney

PERSONNEL MANAGER
Marianne Pinkham

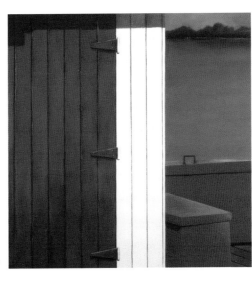

4

FROM THE HELM

PHILIP W. CONKLING

When we sum up the past, we routinely think in terms of time spans in decades—of the sixties, for example, or the fifties, or the thirties. For many of us, however, the decade of the nineties will be forever parenthesized by the numbers nine and eleven of 2001. It is too soon to enumerate all the things we have learned since last September, but a few things are clear. First, we are a nation—admittedly of innumerable disparate traditions, parts and types—but united in ways we hardly imagined possible. Second, the greatness of the nation is directly tied to the greatness of our generosity. Who can ever forget how many people gave, in large ways and small, of their time, blood, sweat and cash to help fill our black pit of despair?

Maine islanders played small but important roles in the massive reconstruction of ourselves as a nation of diverse communities and subcultures. One group, from North Haven, presented the musical "Islands," celebrating Maine island culture to a sold-out audience at a theater in midtown Manhattan as a benefit to the survivors' fund. Jamie Wyeth left his fastness on Southern Island to view the smoking shards of the twin towers and auctioned off his painting, "September 11," of a flag-raising over the ruins, raising over $400,000 for the twin towers fund. No one who saw Wyeth's haunting image or the inspired production of "Islands" will forget how Maine's islanders were able to help transform our collective spirits.

Transforming our individual experiences into a collective recognition of our interconnections is the essence of community. New Yorkers came together as a community after 9/11 and recognized each other's aggressive tenacity in the face of destruction. Islanders perhaps are luckier than most, because an island's sense of community is constantly reinforced by its geographic boundaries.

Strengthening island communities is the collective enterprise of all of us who are drawn to the strange power of islands to unite us across the isolating boundaries of our individual lives. Strong individuals and families are essential to island community life, but they are not sufficient to weather the vagaries of time. Of the hundreds of island communities that disappeared in the late 19th century, most were family islands that simply could not make it on their own. To sustain us over the long haul, we seem to need the rich stew of a community's reinforcing connections.

At the Island Institute, we have begun investing more directly in key elements of island community life. The Island Fellows Program continues to grow in depth and breadth. Fellows work in island schools and libraries; in arts and music programs; in island fisheries research and as staff to island planning committees seeking to preserve the uniqueness of island life. From six last year to twelve today, Island Fellows have become integral parts of the communities they serve. There is no leaving on the last boat; the island is home.

Fellows on North Haven and Islesboro have worked on computer automation of the school and town library card catalogs, so students will be able to search seamlessly in the islands' collections. Island Fellows on Peaks (James Essex and Nate Gray), and Islesboro (Kathleen Reardon) have provided technical staff assistance to various planning initiatives, as these communities try to guide their futures. Jessica Stevens on Monhegan, Nate Geraldi on Vinalhaven and Erin Fisher in Stonington have worked with fishermen and scientists on lobster tagging studies, clam flat and water quality monitoring and a sea scallop enhancement project. Others have worked directly in schools as teachers and have staffed after-school and summer programs on North Haven, Swan's, Cliff, Long and Chebeague. One class of middle school students from Vinalhaven, taught by Island Fellow Mike Felton, is developing a proposal to raise funds to build a community skateboard park.

The Fellows, who are supported by a generous lead grant from the MBNA Foundation, will now also benefit from major support from the William Bingham Charitable Trust, which will endow the first fellowship in rural education. Scores of other individuals who recognize the value of harnessing the idealism of young people to community priorities are also contributing, and the Town of Swan's Island recently voted to allocate funds in its school budget to help fund the community's music teacher, an Island Fellow.

This past year the Institute also initiated the Island Community Fund. Its purpose is to help encourage additional investment in the institutions that make island community life possible. Last year, after adding it all up, we were surprised and pleased to realize that indirectly through the efforts of those here who work with the Island Community Fund, various island organizations and agencies were able to raise over $1.3 million for scholarships, for capital building projects and in school and library grants. A great many individuals and grant-making organizations participated in this largesse. One act of exceptional generosity is Emily Muir's bequest of her estate to the Island Institute and the Maine Community Fund. Her gift will help sustain the island and coastal communities that infused her art, and that of her late husband, sculptor William Muir. We are pleased to have published Emily Muir's memoir, *The Time of My Life*, and to announce the creation of the Emily and William Muir Fund at the Institute, which will help expand the support of the Island Community Fund.

We have also invested in understanding the ecological mechanisms underlying the marine fisheries that are tied to so much of island life. An impoverished ocean surrounding vibrant island communities would be virtually impossible to imagine. This spring we published *Lobsters, Great and Small—How Fishermen and Scientists are Changing Our Understanding of a Maine Icon*. The book grew out of a successful five-year collaboration focused on the dynamics of the lobster populations in Penobscot Bay.

Beyond that collaboration's substantial scientific accomplishments, its real legacy is a deeper trust between the lobstermen who chase and the scientists who study this icon of Maine island life. It was a very risky move five years ago, when the National Oceanic and Atmospheric Administration (NOAA) selected the Institute to administer this complex project, because we were not a research organization. We were beholden neither to the scientific community nor to the fishing community, but we knew both groups well and were respected by each. We can all be proud of the accomplishments of this nationally significant model—solid testimony to the idea that cooperation builds trust.

Looking ahead, we like to think we might be able to predict some of the texture of the next ten years among Maine's island communities and the waters that connect them. We've been following the vicissitudes of island life for 19 years now and have learned a few things along the way, mostly about the wisdom and discipline of active listening. When your role is to help celebrate and contribute to the art and science of island life, a keen eye and ear is more helpful than an active set of vocal chords.

"It's about the *music*"

Can music create community, or is it the other way around?

NATHAN MICHAUD

Jim Conlon (left) and Robin Adair in Conlon's shop. Their group, Sonic Gale (which also includes Harry Ross and Eric Beckman), plays every Thursday ("Except Thanksgiving," says Conlon. "That week we play on Friday."

Photo by Caleb Charland

Around Around 11 in the morning on the Saturday of Labor Day Weekend, people are starting to show up at Jamie Thomas's annual studio party. It's a mix of new and familiar faces, walking down the long dirt driveway, some lugging instruments, some carrying beer.

Jamie and a few others were here early, setting up the staging outside and moving everything onto the lawn. The studio sits back in the woods on 12 acres sloping down to Vinalhaven's southeastern shore. Jamie and his wife, Yvonne, bought the land years ago with intentions of building both the studio—a place for local musicians to gather, practice and record—and a house. The studio has been finished, or at least finished enough to be usable, for a few years, but the house is still on hold ("shows what my priorities are," he says with an ironic grin). The building's about 750 square feet, with a high ceiling, a loft and sound-proofed room below full of mixing and recording equipment. Any other day the studio would be full of instruments and gear (not to mention musicians) but today this stuff is all scattered outdoors.

Vinalhaven, in my mind, has always been associated with music. In my limited time here as a kid I remember music being a part of almost everything. There were always guitars lying about or being passed around. It seemed as if everyone played something. In my travels up and down the coast since, I've heard Vinalhaven identified a few times as the "music island," where just about everyone played and played well. This was my bias when I came here to live, and even as I played saxophone with a couple of the bands I saw little to change my mind.

A blending of bands at Jamie Thomas's studio party last summer (from left) Norm Reidy, his brother Jim Reidy, Bruce Arey, Eric Beckman, Paul Strother and Jeff Killian. Jim Reidy and Strother play in the Boston-area band "Twang," which came to Vinalhaven especially for the studio party. The others are regulars in Vinalhaven's "Barn Ratt."

In his book, *Bowling Alone: The Collapse and Revival of American Community*, Robert Putnam tells the story of the decrease in American civic and social engagement in the last third of the 20th century. The real loss, he says, is the relationships we gain from participation in committees, clubs, bowling leagues, and so forth; these are the bonds that tie us to one another, and provide a sense of connectedness leading to mutual responsibility and ultimately to happy, safe, and well-educated communities. Putnam calls these vital networks "social capital." The book has been a bestseller, apparently prompting people across the country to start looking around, nervously assessing their own stock. At some point, I guess, I started toying with the idea of music on Vinalhaven being an example of an exceptional surplus of "social capital."

That music here is "social," anyhow, is beyond question. Indeed, Jamie's studio has become a kind of social center on Vinalhaven. There are the regular practices of a few bands, of course, which include playing and bull-shooting in nearly equal amounts. But people will also just swing in, to see who might be there, maybe have a beer and strum the guitar a little before heading home. In the summer

you're apt to find someone there at any time of the day or night, playing, listening, sleeping, whatever.

Last summer you were likely to find Jeff Killian, the hand drummer and sternman from Tennessee, pretty much living there when he wasn't out to haul (he practiced so much he had to wrap his hands in duct tape to keep them from bleeding and I'd often find him in there, amid pieces of bloody tape, hitting one drum to the click of a metronome, looking kind of crazed).

Or Norm Reidy, who put a lot of time in the control room last fall with whomever he'd managed to round up, recording tracks for his CD, "Something Simple." He put the vocals and rhythm guitar down himself, then pulled people in one by one to record the other parts. You'd find him in there one day with John "Goog" Arey recording the bass part, another day with Pat Allen doing drums, Joe Nelson for lead guitar, Scott Tolman for a little dobro, and so on until he had 12 original songs filled out, then mixed it all down with a little help from Joe, who has a degree in audio engineering. (Jamie's long-term plan is to keep fitting the studio out until it's professional quality, then enticing bands from away—he suspects this will particularly appeal to city bands—to come out for a week or so, enjoy the island air, maybe do some kayaking and record an album while they're at it. "Though I've probably been holding off on that a little," he says, "because I realize that if people are renting it and recording professionally, then where are we going to play?")

It's kind of hard to talk about a "musical community" here as a distinct sub-

group of the community as a whole. Some play a lot, some play a little, some listen, but many, many take part.

The history of Vinalhaven music and things musical alone could fill volumes. There is the list of home-grown professional musicians, to name a few: Albra Vinal Smith, who graduated from the New England Conservatory at the end of the 19th century and returned to the island to teach and perform; her son, Kilton, who had a successful career playing tuba with the Boston Symphony Orchestra; Leonard Hokanson, an internationally known classical pianist; Mont Arey, who played clarinet for the Detroit Symphony and Rochester Philharmonic; and Bruce Arey, who played pedal-steel guitar with country bands in Washington, D.C., for 20 years.

There are the dances at the Old Memorial Hall downtown (torn down in 1973) and the fanciful-sounding local bands that played there, like Lou's Melody Jazz Trio and the Merry Midnighters. There are the musical theater groups like "Hi-Jinx" and the Island Players. There are the local pickers of the old days like Bob Tolman, Brud Clayter and Sig Beckman—who, it's said, could hold their own with the professional country and dance bands that came to visit. And there's the impressive list of well-known musicians who have summered here over the years.

The 20 or so musicians who frequent the studio are actually only one small part of the larger picture of music on Vinalhaven today. The year-round population of about 1,300 includes classical groups, a marching band, folk duos and trios, vocal groups, church choirs and rock and country bands, all getting together with some

Norm Reidy and the author attempting to record some sax parts for Norm's CD.

degree of regularity to make music. While all the groups don't necessarily occupy the same social space there is a great deal of integration and overlap and, moreover, there seems to be an awareness and shared pride of the musical community as a whole (even among the youngest generation which, some worry, isn't much interested in playing music).

And there are ample opportunities for the ecclectic mix of island groups to share the same venue; last year alone this happened at the Fireman's Picnic at Charlotte Goodhue's, the Block Party downtown, Jamie's studio party, and a benefit concert at the Union Church in March.

Not that different styles always flow together seamlessly. Reverend Michelle Arey-Wiley of the Union Church says planning the concert there—which benefited the Vinalhaven Community Outreach Fund and Families in Crisis—actually sparked a mild controversy because some balked at the prospect of rock and blues being played in a place of worship. In the end, there were some stipulations made about lyrical content: no blatant references to sex or drugs.

"But if you're a blues band, play blues, if you're a rock band play rock, and so on, just edit the lyrics if you have to," Michelle says. "It was a difficult decision, but everyone was very pleased and surprised to see how wonderful it was. Just to see Louise

Bickford, the organist from the church who plays everything from the 1940s and earlier so beautifully, to see her sitting in the third row and tapping her foot to Robin Adair singing 'One Meatball.' How great is that?"

The first Union Church concert was successful enough that it's now repeated during the first week of every March, the stir-crazy time on the island when folks desperately need a reason to get out of the house.

Jamie's studio party started five years ago as simply a summer gathering with music, but it has evolved into a day-long jam session which is as likely to attract performers as listeners. "The first year we had about a hundred people," Jamie says. "Probably ten of those were musicians. The second year we might have had 200, with probably 15 musicians. This year, I didn't advertise it much, so we only got about 65 or 70 people, but I counted and 45 were musicians. I like that ratio. There's still plenty of time for everyone to get up there and play. Our band didn't even play as much as some of the others this year—and that's fine by me. It's not about our band anyway, it's about the music."

At times the event looked more like one continuous performance of a single, constantly changing band than a series of distinct ones, as people came and went, switched instruments and played in different combinations. But what kept it all from sounding confused was one of the unspoken rules of music: play for the song, not for yourself. So that, for example, Jamie's band still sounded like Jamie's band, despite the addition of musicians who had never played with them. At the same time, fresh perspectives added new twists, new layers to old songs, nudging things in new directions while remaining faithful to their original flavor.

And for those less conscious of the etiquette? "You can always weed out the idiots, the ones who hog the stage or whatever," Jamie says. "You know: 'Yuh, nice to know you. Don't come back next year.'"

When Art and Cheryl Lindgren started coming to Vinalhaven for summers, music was a natural way for them to test the social waters here, since he plays bass and she sings and plays guitar. As they played at a couple of fish houses, they got the feeling that they were being sized up, too. "It was really that they were checking us out to see if we would fit," Cheryl says. "It's a good test actually, jamming with people because there's a kind of etiquette to sitting in a circle and playing," Art offers. "If you're tuned into what the other person is trying to do musically while you're playing, it hits a sweet spot that makes you feel really good—but there's always a few guys who just won't give the podium to anyone else."

Having apparently passed the tests, the Lindgrens now live on Vinalhaven full time and are as integrated into the music scene as anyone. Cheryl currently sings

Lou's Melody Trio: Arthur Burns (piano), Leon "Goose" Arey (sax) and Lou Merrithew (drums). One of several bands which used to play for community dances and events. Photo courtesy of Vinalhaven Historical Society.

9

David D. Platt

Building Harps and Musicians on Swan's Island

DAVID D. PLATT

A young teacher who arrived on Swan's Island last year found a rich vein of musical interest already in place. In nine months as an Island Institute Fellow there, Candyce Dunham has energized that interest, creating ensembles for voice, harp, bagpipes and percussion. Some of the groups are connected with the island elementary school, where she teaches half-time; others are made up of community members and students who have signed up for private lessons. Dunham is also teaching violin to at least two students, and several people are taking guitar lessons.

"There was a school assembly right after we came here in September [2001]," says Dunham, a harpist trained at the Eastman College of Music in Rochester, N.Y. "I played harp while people ate desserts." She described the various instruments on which she could provide lessons, and circulated a sign-up sheet.

The results were as good as anyone had a right to expect. Sixteen adults signed up for a chorus that began preparing for a Christmas concert. Others joined a "show choir" and began working on song-and-dance routines. Nineteen "very anxious students" signed up for a harp group and 20 for a percussion ensemble. Dunham signed up a dozen people for piano lessons; seven kids for "twinklers," a music-through-movement program; and seven for "terrific twos," a rhythm program for very young children. Bagpipe and string lessons got underway too. At school, Dunham began teaching music composition to three different age groups.

In December the entire school (34 students), all three teachers and a chorus of 23 all took part in a well-attended Christmas concert, complete with Santa, who pulled gifts for everyone from his apparently bottomless sack. A second concert, planned for spring, was to feature original compositions by Dunham's school students, as well as bagpipers and harpists.

Planning for the harp ensemble prompted some particularly original thinking. A harp—even one for a beginning student—is an elaborate instrument with strings, pedals and sounding board that can cost thousands of dollars. Candyce brought her own harp to the island last fall, but providing others for students seemed beyond everyone's reach—until her husband, Ben, a skilled woodworker ("he can make anything," Candyce says), suggested that he build harps for the students. Through the Island Institute the Dunhams applied for grant funding to buy materials, and by late winter Ben was at work on two harps in his home shop. Cost: about one-third that of a store-bought harp.

ing-rock-n'-roll-there" speeches, it does occur to me that success in both things relies on achieving the same remarkable feat: being as much of an individual as possible while still complementing the group. Or, put another way: letting the needs of the group help you realize your individuality.

If you've ever joined in singing a hymn at a church where you know the whole congregation, then you know what I'm trying to get at. Listening, even with your eyes shut, you can pick out each voice and attach a face to it, and usually a profession, a demeanor and a history. The whole thing can become an almost unbearably rich social tapestry: complete personalities for a few moments, condensed into sound, each individual trying to complement the others, so that by that magic of the collective spirit the whole is more than the sum of the parts. As with any such endeavor, the goal of perfect harmony is never quite reached—a few flat, a few sharp, a few too loud, a few too showy with their harmonizing. But it's the good intentions of the whole thing that matter, the reaching for the right pitch, the goal of creating something where in one sense individuals are subsumed by the voice of the whole, while the very act of striving for this somehow creates a sense of individualism. In this sense the song, or more precisely the singing—stragglers and all—is perfect.

Music, then, can work as a kind of release valve: it allows people to socialize in a context free of the stickiness of everyday issues, while reinforcing those basic skills that will be absolutely necessary to getting things done when the music stops. To put it in the language of *Bowling Alone*, music both "bridges" and "bonds": it brings together people who might not come together otherwise, and it reinforces an already existing identity and sense of tradition.

"Music is the ultimate bridge of language and culture barriers," Jamie says. We're sitting on a couple of folding chairs in the middle of the studio, the tape recorder on a conga drum between us. Bruce Arey, who plays pedal steel with Jamie's band (Barn Rat, they're called—an acronym formed with the first letters of the members' last names), is a few feet away, listening and smoking. "It doesn't make any difference where you're from—a C is a C."

"Last summer," Bruce offers, "we had Irish music, French music, Indian music. You name it, we had it."

"Yeah," Jamie says. "Some of it isn't necessarily anything I'd buy a CD of and sit down and listen to, but that doesn't matter. The more variety the bet-

twice a week with bassist Eric Beckman and string player Scott Tolman (members of two of Vinalhaven's more musical families, sort of like royalty), with an eye toward coffee shop and restaurant gigs both on and off the island. She also joins her daughter, Britta, in singing back-up vocals in Richie Carlson's rock band.

This summer Art and Cheryl helped bring back the weekly open-mike nights at the Mill Race coffee shop. "The main thing is it's fun," Cheryl says, "and how often do you get to have fun these days?" Clearly, the importance of such times to the people who participate is beyond question. Cheryl recalls the fishhouse days: "These guys would play until two o'clock in the morning and they're up at three or four. They'd basically just turn around and go back out and fish—but music was just that important to them."

The more I spoke with people, the more I started to think about the similarities between playing music in a group and living in a small town. While I'll spare us both the tedium of talk about "microcosms" or "everything-I-need-to-know-about-living-on-Vinalhaven-I-learned-playter. [Music] has been a good thing here to get summer people and island people together and not at each others' throats—it's worked out well, really."

Music may act as a social bridge between islanders and visitors (I certainly have it to thank for many of my friendships here), but it also closes gaps within the community. Several people said they play music with people they probably wouldn't hang out with otherwise, for whatever reason. Music seems to work across occupation, social tastes (i.e., to party or not), generations—almost everything.

Bruce, for instance, is almost 30 years older than most of the Barn Ratt regulars. When Jamie knocked on his door it had been 13 years since Bruce had packed up his pedal steel guitar and headed back to Vinalhaven to care for his mother after playing bars and honky-tonks in Washington, D.C., for a quarter-century.

"He didn't know who I was, so I told him who my father was, and my grandfather, and then he figured it out. I said, 'It'd be nice if you came down and played with us sometime, if you wouldn't mind.' He said, 'Well, I haven't played for four or five years, in fact I haven't even taken it out of the box.' So I said, 'Well, don't you think it's about time?' About six weeks later I finally convinced him to come down. He said, 'Well, I don't know if I know anything you boys know, but I'll see what I can do.' "

As luck would have it, the band—at that point Jamie, Goog and Norm—favored some of the old country songs Bruce used to play anyway. Not that it really would have mattered. "He said he had a little rust," Jamie recalls, "but even with a little rust he was better than us. And once the rust came off, he was just blowing us away."

"Course then they start springing some good ones on me," Bruce says, "like the Pink Floyd." Jamie laughs: "The time Goog played some Pink Floyd—Bruce was playing right along with it, just like he knew it. At the end he says 'well, that wasn't Hank Williams but it wasn't bad. What was it?' and Goog says 'Pink Floyd' and Bruce says 'Well, it could've been Purple Magnolia for all I know, but I liked it all right.' "

Given the wealth of music I've seen here, I was initially surprised to hear concerns about the future (though in retrospect this in itself is testament to its importance over the years). But opinions differ. On the one hand, the island has several talented and motivated music teachers and plenty of kids taking lessons of one sort or another. On the other, the band scene in general has fluctuated in recent years and some worry that there there's not a lot of motivation among school kids to form bands on their own.

"Part of the reason why I built this," Jamie says, gesturing to the walls around him, "is that I'd seen that music was pretty much gone on the island. I mean, there were people out there playing instruments, but there weren't many bands playing out, people weren't playing in bands. Years ago there were four or five bands going on any Saturday night. It has gotten a little better now, and I hope it continues. It would be nice to see more teenagers getting involved, doing something other than hanging out on Main Street and getting in trouble. This is a safe environment for them, as long as they behave themselves. I think music will come back if it's given the chance."

When I talked with a handful of high-schoolers who have started using the studio as practice space, they admitted that few of their classmates were interested in playing in groups. While they tended to blame the usual suspects—technology, mass media—it wasn't the familiar TV-rots-your-brain-and-leaves-you-slack-jawed-and-apathetic argument. It was simpler: first of all, playing music is no longer necessary as a form of hanging out. You can buy better music than you could play, and you can listen to it anywhere, any time, and there are other things you can do with friends these days—watching TV, playing video games, whatever. And the kids point out that styles of popular music have changed: "Back in the 70s they didn't have all this rap and hip-hop," says sophomore bass player Eric Beckman, while allowing that his tastes are more like those of his fellow bassist and dad, Eric Sr.: 70s rock n' roll.

"At some point people just put down the real instruments," his classmate, guitarist Farley Mesko, adds. "Music has become more and more manufactured. The airwaves are clogged with all this recycled stuff. People think of music as MTV now—nobody takes it any further."

What if Vinalhaven lost its band scene? The question forced my hand: what role does music play in the community? "I don't know if it's unique—I've never lived in any other community," says Phil

Caleb Charland

Bruce Arey (son of "Goose" Arey from Lou's Melody Trio) played pedal steel professionally in Washington, D.C., for 25 years before returning to Vinalhaven.

Crossman, who sings tenor in "Phil and the Blanks" and other vocal groups. "But it certainly is a big part of things out here. As it is, for that matter, on North Haven and Matinicus." Basically, his answer was like several others I heard: compared to what?

Robert Putnam says we need to recreate social networks like the musical scene here in order to regain the benefits of community and, ultimately, the health of our nation. But isn't that a heavy load to put on Vinalhaven, a place which after all is not without problems of its own? In the end I'm left wondering if there isn't a danger in terms like "social capital." Because to isolate something like music on Vinalhaven—something which grew and continues to grow naturally, to a certain extent out of necessity, in a context of shared geography, history, ancestry and industry—to call this an asset is to think separately about something that can never be separated, that can't exist out of context. *Bowling Alone* says that social networks like a music scene create community. While its social benefits to the island are obvious, I've learned the importance of remembering that on Vinalhaven, at least, community created the music scene.

Nathan Michaud is program officer for community planning at the Island Institute. He lives on Vinalhaven.

The *Spirit* of the Grass

*With 400 wild horses, how could life on
North America's remotest island ever get lonely?*

KATIE VAUX

Zoe Lucas sits quietly in the dune grass. It rises and falls around her in waves of mottled green. It is lush and sharp, and conceals the crest of a 70-foot sand dune that rises steeply out of the Atlantic ocean. Nearby, six wild horses graze: a black stallion, a bay-colored juvenile male, two chestnut mares and two chocolate foals. Zoe silently observes them as they migrate toward and away from each other, dictated by the direction of their grazing and their proximity to one another.

A curious mare slowly approaches Zoe. She is a light chestnut color, a young mother with a round belly, a plump rear and a thick blaze of white running down her face. She puts one hoof in front of the other, slowly but deliberately, until she is within inches of Zoe. Then gently, she lowers her neck and touches Zoe's face with her nose. The two of them stay there for a long moment, exploring each other's personal space.

This kind of encounter is not routine for Zoe, but it is not uncommon either. She has lived the last 30 years on Sable Island. A self-taught biologist, she abandoned a successful career as a goldsmith in Halifax to live on a sparsely inhabited sand bar 160 kilometers southeast of Nova Scotia.

Eventually, man-made structures fill with sand.

Sable Island is a crescent moon of sand just over a kilometer wide, but curving 45 kilometers long. It begins with sand spits, then rises ominously into dunes that loom more than three stories above the water. The island, whose name comes from the French word for sand, is remote. It has a comprehensive collection of shipwrecks and recovered treasure. There are stories of ghosts who prowl the dunes. The island is also known for its biological uniqueness: it is home to a rare species of freshwater sponge, two unique species of insects, and it is the only known breeding ground for the Ipswich Sparrow. More recently, the island has gained notoriety for the conflict surrounding the exploration and drilling for oil and gas along its shoals.

Most of all, Sable is known for the wild horses that live and graze on its dunes. For Zoe Lucas, this is the most important reason to live on Sable Island, and she has devoted her life to the study of one of the last known populations of wild horses to live entirely without human intervention.

These days, getting to Sable Island is no small task. Anyone traveling to Sable must get permission from the Canadian Coast Guard, and prove they have just reason to be visiting the island and adequate ground support once there. The island has no medical resources, fire department or emergency crew; an accident on Sable can quickly become an emergency.

Flights to the island are prohibitively expensive, and the weather often makes beach landings impossible. The only plane that flies to Sable carries a maximum of six passengers, although seats are usually filled with supplies for the only two people who live here year-round, Zoe Lucas and the manager of island's atmospheric research and weather station.

Historically, records show that getting to Sable Island wasn't all that difficult; the challenge was getting there intentionally. Two hundred twenty-two shipwrecks have been recorded on Sable since 1801, and the island is known as "The Graveyard of the Atlantic." Historians estimate the number of shipwrecks over time at about 500, with thousands of lives lost.

The most influential factor lending Sable to shipwreck is its location directly in the confluence of two great ocean currents: the frigid Labrador Current, and the Gulf Stream, whose tropical waters warm the eastern coast of North America, Britain and Norway. This confluence creates intensely thick and damp fog, as well as strange localized currents. Strong winds blow in all directions, resulting in extremely treacherous and unpredictable conditions.

The fog that surrounds Sable an average of 125 days a year together with the island's constantly moving shoals made it a deadly hazard for even the most seasoned and wary sailors. For those caught in a storm, shipwreck on Sable was almost a certainty. Sable's shoals run 20 miles out, and like waves, they rise and fall and are constantly moving, making charts unreliable. In a National Geographic article written in 1965, author Melville Bell

Grosvenor recounts spending days trying to plot a course to approach the island, becoming lost by fog and false horizon, and then the exhausting work of mooring his yawl without driving it into a submerged sand bank. Although Sable is anchored to the continental shelf, maps of the island confirm that since its discovery in 1500, it has shrunk in size, and may have moved eastward.

For me, as for some of the early settlers who came to the island 300 years ago, going to Sable is the adventure of a lifetime. Flying out on a fixed-wing propeller plane, it's an hour and a half before the island rises out of the open Atlantic. From nowhere, its enormous stark white dunes come out of the sea, towering over the deep blue water. As the plane begins to descend, thousands of sunbathing seals scatter into the water. From the air, I can see bands of wild horses grazing, a few small structures on the island and the crumbling foundations of other structures lost over time to wind and sand. As we come closer and closer, I realize that I cannot not see a single tree, or boulder, or handful of brown earth. Just sand and grass. Slowly, the pilot brings the plane down on a strip of beach squeezed between dunes and waves, both bigger than the plane itself. A band of grazing horses acknowledge our arrival, and then continue their meal.

When I step out of the loud, sterile body of the plane, my head is encased by the salt-soaked air and the roar of waves, glistening and pounding on the shore beside me. As I would find out, there is never a time or a place on the island where I cannot hear the sea.

Zoe greets me. She is a small woman, almost elfin in appearance, with bright eyes and a ready smile. She is to the point, and happy. Apart from walking, her only means of transportation on the island is a one-person ATV. Stray bones, bird wings, a horse skull and a knife stick awkwardly out of a crate strapped to the back.

"I've been here 30 years," she tells me. "My entire adult life." She straddles the ATV and turns the key to start it. "I don't even have my driver's license!"

We leave the south beach, where the plane landed, and cross the width of the island in just minutes. Vehicles on the island are restricted to ATVs, tractors and the weather station truck, which is mounted on tracks instead of tires. Island roads are sandy ruts cut through dune grass, and are highly controlled to prevent damage to the dunes, or the plant and animal life they host.

Even on the clearest of days, like today, no other land is visible from Sable. Cruising down the north beach, we could be on any tropical island: the sand is platinum, and the clear blue waves move in tandem as the water becomes deeper and bluer. Zoe carefully negotiates her way past huge colonies of Harbor and Gray Seals sunning themselves. As we pass, they flop towards the water, chopping the surf into boils of sand and foam. With their heads bobbing in the eight-foot swells, hundreds of black eyes consume us until we pass. The water is warm, but not fit for swimming: it is home to several species of sharks who feed on seals. Both living and dead seals along the beach bear scythe-shaped marks of shark predation.

Along the beach, the island begins to reveal itself to me. To our left, the crashing surf. To our right, massive dunes that hide the sun. They are capped by dune grass, and prickly, low-growing vegetation. Shifted and shaped by the wind, the dunes end abruptly, falling 30 feet down into sculpted white sand blowouts, valleys created as dunes pull away from each other. These white valleys are hot and bright and difficult to walk through. Sand gives way with every step. Surrounding me are dozens of sun-bleached skulls, ribs and vertebrae, slowly being buried by sand. Scattered among them are the remains of human objects lost to the tide and found to Sable.

On the far end of this blowout, a band of horses gather by a water hole. Using their hooves, they dig into the fresh-water "lens" that lies underneath the island and provides drinking water for both horses and humans. Slowly, they meander towards the beach, passing us without pausing.

Zoe Lucas has devoted her life to the study of one of the last known populations of wild horses to live entirely without human intervention.

Back on the beach, we stop at the decomposed body of a horse. It died lying on its side in the sand, and has not been moved since. After a horse dies, Zoe notes its location, and leaves it for gulls and maggots to eat the flesh and digest. Now all that is left is the bones and the tough, dry leather fastening them together. Sand has filled in the depressions that used to be round with muscle. This is the collapsed shell of a stallion.

Zoe hops off the ATV with a short, sharp knife and cuts the skull away from the body. She places it in a woven plastic bag, and straps it onto the front rack of her vehicle. She will take measurements of the skull and add the data to her long-term study of the horses.

"This horse was a band stallion. I don't know how he died. One day he was in fine health, and the next day I found him here, dead," she says. This kind of sudden, inexplicable death is very uncommon, she adds.

Zoe talks about the horses in both very personal and very scientific terms. She discusses their individual personalities while pointing out a mare she doesn't expect to survive the winter. She makes no assumptions about their capabilities or limitations.

Zoe first came to Sable Island in the early 1970s, while studying painting and goldsmithing at the Nova Scotia College of Art and Design.

"I was stunned by how beautiful it was," she recalls. "Everything was reduced to very essential greens and blues, with splashes of color from bands of horses and colonies of seals. But I didn't want to paint it. The island is far more interesting than a painting. I didn't just want to observe it. I wanted to integrate myself into it."

Sable's herd of horses descends from animals left there in the 1750s.

After making four or five trips to the island as a volunteer, Zoe began working summers on a dune restoration project funded by Mobil. Over time, she found herself observing the horses, and compiling the data she recorded. This led into other work, including projects on Harp and Hooded seals, shark predation and oiled bird surveys. She continued working part time on the island while earning her masters degree in goldsmithing, and later teaching the same subject at the college. By the early 1980s, she had spent nearly ten years working part time on the island. That was when she made the decision to leave her steady job to live year-round on the island and pursue her independent research.

"I was not thinking I would be here for good," she recalls. "There was no big plan. I just wanted to be here. I was more interested in Sable than anything else. I couldn't resist the intellectual challenge it presented: to learn directly from the source, instead of from books."

She pauses, then continues. "I was attracted to its gentleness in space; not cluttered with the activities of people."

The first people to arrive on the island were the Portuguese, who brought cattle and pigs here in the 16th century. One hundred years later, French settlers brought the first horses. In 1738, Reverend Le Mercier reported that there were no animals left on the island. That was soon to change: that same year, he

brought horses to the island as part of his farming operation. He left the island 15 years later, and it is not known whether all of his animals were removed, or by whom. What is known is that shortly thereafter, between 1755 and 1760, Thomas Hancock, a Boston merchant, brought a large herd of horses to the island (animals that most likely belonged to the recently expelled Acadians). When Hancock died in 1764, his plan to ship the pasturing horses to the West Indies had not come to fruition, and the horses stayed.

By domestic standards, Sable Island horses look shaggy. Their manes are long and tangled and bleached by the sun. Their winter coats are thick and soft and disheveled. They are descended from a

collection of breeds, and Zoe attributes their compact, stocky build to the need for the most efficient way of maintaining body heat.

The number of horses on the island has ranged, over the years, from 200 to 400. They have neither died off nor over-populated. Currently, there about 400 horses, divided among 45 bands. Bands can be as small as one stallion and one mare, but they can also be much larger. Family bands can be made up of one or two stallions, a number of mares, foals and juvenile males. Bands sometimes split when a juvenile male steals a mare for himself and creates a new band. Stallions often battle for control of a band.

In the past, Sable Island horses were routinely rounded up, and those who could be captured were sent to the mainland to be sold. When Alexander Graham Bell visited the island in 1898, vainly searching for friends whose boat was wrecked on the island, he took three horses back with him. In the past few decades, islanders can recall visitors attempting to lasso horses, trying to ride them, trying to feed them and even trying to take them home.

In the late 1950s, the Government of Canada voted to sell off the horses of Sable Island. After much controversy, the decision was reversed, and the government instead passed laws protecting the horses from all human interference.

Do Sable Island horses have a better life than domestic horses? "They suffer remarkably fewer respiratory diseases," says Zoe. "It may be because they spend all their lives outside." The horses are healthier than domestic horses, she feels, because they are not managed. Domesticated horses don't live in groups the way the wild horses of Sable do, she explains. Her observations have demonstrated how horses have preferences for companions, and for particular bands. "All horses have psychological and emotional relationships that the wild horses on Sable are able to play out," she says.

We continue on along the north beach, moving further and further east. The dunes here rise higher and fall more steeply than others on the island, reaching 90 feet before diminishing into a spit of sand that trails on for five kilometers, then disappearing into the sea.

Zoe pulls the ATV over to inspect a small, soft, doll-like creature on the beach. She squats down next to it and strokes its belly.

"Come over and look," she beckons.

I approach and see a tiny, aborted gray seal fetus. Its body is still warm, but its eyes have been pecked out by gulls. Its silvery fur is rich and silky.

"Feel the flippers," she urges.

They are smooth and soft, and I can feel all the tiny bones within. They feel like human hands. She turns the fetus over, and the skull cap falls away, revealing a small cranium, soaked in blood. Within a few hours, its cream-colored belly will be excavated by predatory birds.

"After all" she says with a smile, "a gull's gotta eat!"

Nearing the eastern tip of the island, we have left the dunes behind and cruise out over the spit, which lies only a few meters above the water, and is less than half a kilometer wide. I can see both "sides" of the island in one glance, as well as parts of the spit where the tide has washed over, carrying away any marine litter or animals in its way. Once while cruising along this spit, a high tongue of surf washed under Zoe, floating her ATV and taking it out to sea. She escaped the vehicle before she too was lost to the tide.

Stretching nearly five kilometers, this part of the island has a startling psychological impact on me. I feel vulnerable, desolate. There is no grass out here, and no horses, just the howling wind that steals warmth from my body. The beach is streaked with veins of red mineral sands that from a distance look like thick rivers of blood dripping across the white spit and into the water. It is a clear day, but the enormous, intimidating dunes have suddenly disappeared in the distance until all I can see is this spit of sand, and the thousand ways a person like me could die out here. I suddenly crave to be back among the dunes, where horses suffer the weather with no shelter, but are at least

safe from these rip tides that crash against each other in the tumultuous remains of the North American continent. I cling tightly to Zoe, and her simple presence anchors my psychological composure.

We are stopping often along the spit, as Zoe scans the beach for oiled sea birds, part of a project funded by Mobil. We also stop each time we pass a deflated child's balloon, which she picks up and tucks into her crate. This is part of an independent marine litter survey she has been conducting over the past 3 years. In her living quarters, she has stacks of boxes filled with a confetti of decrepit balloons and ribbons. She explains that she counts balloons by the circular nib where they are blown and tied, rather than by balloon fragments she finds.

"A fragment isn't a reliable way to count them, because one balloon could have many fragments, whereas each balloon has only one opening," she explains. When on the mainland, she gives presentations at elementary schools, talking to kids about what happens to their balloons when they let go of them, whether at a party or at a deliberate balloon release.

"I want kids to know what happens to their balloons. They don't have many opportunities to make a difference in their world, but this way, they can at least make the decision whether they want to have balloons at their parties or not," she says.

Being the only land for hundreds (if not thousands) of miles in almost every direction, Sable catches enormous tides of human refuse. Marine litter on Sable consists of everything from pop cans and garbage bags to television sets, computers, stoves, freezers, channel markers, marine flares, boat equipment and the occasional

message in a bottle. Zoe once found a prosthetic leg buried vertically in beach sand, the bottom of its foot facing the sky.

"I was less afraid of the prosthetic leg than I feared somebody might be attached to it—which they were not," she says. "I kept that leg for a while. I would leave it somewhere in a room, and somehow it would move to another spot, although I was always sure I hadn't moved it. I finally got rid of it."

The most noteworthy piece of marine litter to wash ashore on Sable Island happened in the early 1990s, when $2.5 million worth of cocaine was found on the north beach.

"Once we realized what it was inside all these little sealed baggies, we were quite anxious to get rid of them," recalls the manager of the island's weather station. "We didn't want the bad guys coming looking for it."

In times past, more than refrigerators and buoys washed ashore on Sable. It was people, and the vessels that carried them.

Original settlers, both intentional and those who had escaped their wrecked ships to find themselves stranded on Sable, lived on salvaged provisions, vegetables they could grow, and the animals that grazed on the dunes. In 1801, the Governor of Nova Scotia, alarmed by reports that "a man and woman of wicked character" were inhabiting Sable "for the infamous, inhumane purpose of plundering, robbing and causing shipwrecks," sent a scout to investigate the island. Instead of finding depraved marauders, the scout sent back word that Sable was inhabited by a few poor souls, and that the island was in desperate need of people willing to aid

Continued on page 55

Being the only land for hundreds (if not thousands) of miles in almost every direction, Sable catches enormous tides of human refuse.

17

A Bowline

in the Dark

*William Thon didn't retire
when his sight failed him
—he changed his palette*

William Thon in his studio.

Facing page: *The Herring Fleet*, ca 1963, oil on panel, 22" x 47"

STEVE CARTWRIGHT

Bill Thon and four friends once bought a fishing schooner and sailed from New York to a remote Pacific island. In this youthful and far-fetched enterprise, they were ostensibly pursuing legendary buried treasure. Perhaps they were just seeing the world. "I was young and the world was my oyster," said Thon, seven decades later, as we sat in his sun-swept Port Clyde living room—a room with a view out to sea that he no longer saw.

Thon and his buddies never found gold, but William Thon found himself as an artist, and has left behind a great legacy of sea paintings. And Thon surprised nearly everyone when he left an estate of about $7 million, the bulk of it given to the Portland Museum of Art, which mounted a spring 2002 retrospective of the artist's work. Rockland's Farnsworth museum received a gift of $100,000. Thon died at home in December 2000. He was 94. His wife of 70 years, Helen, died one year earlier.

*William and Helen Thon aboard
the* AQUAVELLE.

Beset with near-blindness toward the end of his life, Thon painted some of his finest, most elementally powerful works when his eyes could only pick out blurry, peripheral shapes. He couldn't see colors. But his inner vision remained sharply focused, evocatively expressed in black-and-white washes and powerful, minimal lines that bore into the soul.

Thon kept on sailing his Friendship sloop, ECHO, taking a turn around the harbor as long he was able. He pointed out that he practically knew the way by smell. Besides, all the fishermen knew Bill. More than a few local households have original Thon works, given by the artist.

Thon called Helen his "right arm" and she said that made her important since that was the arm he painted with; the couple lived frugally in the shipshape house and studio they built on a field now framed by tall trees. A visitor might be handed a glass of sherry, or invited to sample Helen's cooking. The Thon homestead was purchased by artist Jamie Wyeth and his wife, Phyllis, who knew and liked Thon, and has since been put on the market again, minus its waterfront.

Thon imbued his paintings with spiritual energy and a sensual immediacy. His paintings of boats and the sea, of quarries and birches and seasonal changes, are visual poems.

Art historian Susan Larsen of Tenants Harbor, in an essay for the Portland exhibit, said Thon "stands apart from many of Maine's artistic heroes. Winslow Homer, Marsden Hartley, Andrew Wyeth and others would place man at the center of their dramatic imagery, while using nature as an accompaniment and a significant factor in human affairs. William Thon's embrace of

the full force of the physical world is an act of unusual courage and faith in the inherently spiritual nature of the universe…"

When Thon had full eyesight, he painted in oils, but he increasingly shifted to watercolors in the latter part of his life. He evolved—perhaps "invented" is a better word—his own special technique of swirling, sponged washes, combining ink and water for a "resist" effect. He saturated the paper on which he painted, working quickly, deftly.

On my last visit a few weeks before his death, Thon sat with his 5 o'clock vodka in hand. He seemed delighted to recall boyhood summers camping on a Staten Island beach, painting a raw tent canvas with limited success—but at six or seven years old, it was a brave start.

The sea called to him, as it did all his life starting with boyhood summers on Staten Island, when he would row to West Bank Light or Romer Shoals Light with magazines for the keepers to read. And the sea called in his final shore-bound days when he would reach for his binoculars and try to figure out what sort of boat was passing by. "It was like looking through waxed paper," he said.

Thon's most striking and impressionistic work involves bold strokes in black and white, using his peculiar wet-paper technique involving brushes, sponges, a razor and India ink pen. He captures the seasons, particularly the stark clarity of the woods in winter; and always the sea, painted in all her moods, from flat calm to furious gale. "I do about half my work by instinct," he said. "You know, a sailor used to be able to throw an eye splice or a bowline in the dark."

The sea infused his work and his heart. In Thon's faith, the ocean is pretty close to the Almighty. "There is something deeply religious about it," he said. "It is a mystical,

powerful force that I regard as superhuman, somehow; a force that I try to interpret with what meager tools we have."

Thon was not religious in conventional terms. At the artist's memorial service, the Rev. Mark Reinhardt said Bill would faithfully drive his wife to the Catholic church, then sit in the car waiting for her. Father Reinhardt suggested Thon expressed his faith through art, through his affection for Port Clyde and its people.

Thon valued the opinions of fishermen as much as those of any critics in New York, where he grew up and where for decades his work was handled by Midtown Galleries. One of those friends was lobsterman Syd Davis, whose wharf is next to Thon's property. Thon used to say he would quit painting when Davis quit lobstering. "I'm not going to retire 'til Syd does." Davis hauled his boat the day of Thon's funeral, and gave it to his son.

Earlier, Davis brought over the last two lobsters he caught, giving them to Thon and his adoring caregiver of the last years of his life, Heidi Stevens of Rockland.

Sometimes, on visits to the hospital, people would ask Thon when he had retired. "I'm not," he would say. When near the end he was told he needed to stay in the hospital, he said no, he was going home, and that's what he did, helped by Stevens.

"I have always had a real low self-esteem. Bill built me up so I felt good about me," said Stevens, who said Thon told her if he was 20 years younger he would marry her. Before Helen Thon died, she made Stevens promise to stay with Bill for the rest of his life. She did, and Thon left her several paintings and the Red Baron, his Oldsmobile.

"He and I used to go on picnics quite often in the Red Baron. He was my best buddy, he was my confidant," she said. "He gave me a painting of Bill Thon, the only painting he had done of himself. He gave it to me eight months before he died. He thought it was hideous, but it was so Bill."

"He used to sit there and talk about the birds in Rome, the buildings in Rome and how strong and powerful they were. He said that he used to just love to touch them, because they were so old. Nothing bored Bill, and I sure as hell didn't. I kept him on his toes. I used to tell him all the time that he was my Cary Grant." Thon grew fond not only of Stevens, but of her pint-size Yorkie, a dog the size of a cat.

Once, Stevens watched Thon at work, and was amazed at how he created a picture in minutes, and how that experience enlivened the artist, too.

Cynthia Hyde, who with her husband, Jim Kinnealey, handles Thon's artwork at Rockland's Caldbeck Gallery, remembered

how Bill and Helen would walk hand in hand down Main Street, sporting berets. She said Thon's art is charged with life, as well as with his love for Maine and the sea.

Norm Tate, fellow Port Clyde artist and sailor, said of his long-time close friend, "Bill painted from his heart. Really, what he painted was his reaction to what he saw, and he had an incredible memory to carry what he had seen and elevate it. What he did you could never photograph. It had gone through the filter of his mind and heart. He was not affected by what the fashion was in the art field. He had his own way of looking at things and was faithful to it."

Becoming an artist against the odds of the Depression was a little crazy, but perhaps an artist needs to be a little crazy, Tate suggested. "Bill went his own way in painting, and in everything else. He did not want to become a surrealist or even an abstract expressionist. He took his own path."

When Thon's eyesight began to fail, Tate said, "it was the worst kind of macular degeneration. One day he could see and the next day he couldn't. Everything was sort of a brownish-red. Most artists would go into a decline. What did he do? He changed his palette. Bill has been not only a lesson to us, to appreciating art, but he has also been a lesson to us in his acceptance of adversity."

Thon wrote that "painting is largely a matter of the spirit, and that the eyes and hands of the artist and the tools of his trade must be made to obey it ... no doubt the character of an artist, or at least his interests, are reflected in the things that he collects around him. My studio is filled with paintings, prints, sculptured objects, boat models that I have made, colorful stones, bits of bark, weathered wood, and other incidental objects whose form, color or texture have attracted me enough to bring them up to the house."

In a 1997 interview, Thon described himself as a self-taught artist. "I've delighted in that I didn't have [formal training]. I didn't have to unlearn some style of a master." In 1925, he left after one month at The Art Students League of New York, because, he said, he was stuck in a beginners' class. Perhaps his independent spirit had something to do with it.

Although he rejected art school for himself, he encouraged one young protege to take that route. Freedom Hamlin, Heidi Stevens' daughter, wasn't sure what to do when she began taking lessons from the master, just months before he died. Now 21 and a student at Maine College of Art, she is the only student Thon ever tutored.

"William Thon gave me the confidence I needed at a critical point in my life," Hamlin said.

Broad Reach, 1978, watercolor, 25" x 40". Photo courtesy of the Caldbeck Gallery, Rockland.

Thon found endless inspiration in ships. "I've seen hundreds of them in New York Harbor," he said in a March 2000 interview. "There was part of the harbor set aside for the sailing ships when I was a boy. And even when I was a young man, I used to see them when I went to work on the ferry every day. They were usually loaded with lumber, and the deck was awash, practically. They were usually four-masters. This would have been in the '30s."

Thon said he admired yachts, but they lacked the authenticity, the grit of a commercial vessel "with salt all over it."

In his final year he kept a less rigorous painting schedule; he worked in his studio when he felt like it. But it was important to keep working. "I can't do anything else, and the alternative is to just sit here all day and listen to the radio, which is not very productive." He painted a couple of boats. "To a small degree I can see. I don't see any detail. But I work with big brushes."

Steve Cartwright *writes regularly for Island Institute publications.*

LOCAL Knowledge

There is more than one way to bring a ship into port

Story by
NAOMI SCHALIT

Photographs by
CHRISTOPHER AYRES

It's seven A.M., and Jeff Cockburn has just pulled his Volvo into the parking lot at the Searsport town landing. Wayne Hamilton's got his boat waiting at the dock to ferry Cockburn out to the IZ, a Croation-owned and crewed tanker lying at anchor in Searsport Harbor. Crows cry sharply overhead, and the sun is just rising over a windless day. It's flat calm out on the water. Cockburn, armed with a backpack, climbs onto Hamilton's immaculate boat—a boat that bristles with the kind of electronics Hamilton sells just inshore from here, at Hamilton Marine. Cockburn reaches for the marine radio, which is squawking in the background. It's time to establish contact with the ship. "Motor Tanker IZ, Searsport Pilot boat channel one-six." A Croation-accented strangling sound comes back as the reply. "Yessir, good morning," says Cockburn. "Switch to channel 10 please." This time the answer's more clear.

Jeff Cockburn aboard the pilot boat.

"Hokay, one-zeeero. Yessir, we're just here off your starboard side making the approach, so we'll be alongside shortly," says Cockburn. "Hokay, Roger Roger." If you dressed the 40-year-old Cockburn just right, with a big gold hoop earring and an eyepatch, the dark-haired and ruddy pilot would easily pass as a pirate. But dressed in a knit vest and silk tie, Cockburn looks more the part of a businessman than a mariner. Cockburn is a graduate of Maine Maritime Academy, and he shipped out for 13 years.

"I started out working on oceanographic ships up in the Arctic and in the South Pacific," says Cockburn. "Then went to work on oil tankers for eight or nine years and got some good big ship experience. It was exciting when I first started to do the travel and all of a sudden wake up in a new country and learn a little bit about how the rest of the world works. But then you have a family, and sometimes being away for three, four months at a time loses its appeal."

Hungry for home, he returned to Maine. A ship's pilot job is what many merchant mariners dream of when they're away from home, says Cockburn. "To be able to do the same type of work, working on ships, handling ships, and doing it here locally is a pretty sweet deal. And it arguably may be the most challenging aspect of that kind of industry, you're doing the ship docking, you're undocking, you're handling the ship in close-quarter situations, you're doing coastal land navigation instead of ocean passages." So Cockburn became one of four partners in the Penobscot Bay and River Pilots' Association.

Capt. Billy Abbott of Belfast, the veteran Penobscot pilot to whom Cockburn apprenticed while learning to be a pilot, respects the skills of Cockburn and his fellow Penobscot River pilots. But he worries that their reliance on fancy electronics could spell trouble. This from a man who learned piloting before the days of even radar. "They should learn the river without any of the aids at all," says Abbott firmly. What would happen if all their electronics went on the fritz? he asks. "When I had a new pilot, I'd cover up the radar, and he learned the river without looking in the radar. And that's the way it should be today."

For decades, Abbott brought ships and barges up and down the Penobscot River. He dodged ledges and shoals, used his wits in an era when that was about as technological as you got, and shared meals with men who came from all corners of the globe. But this past year, he hung up his captain's hat after what he calculates as 3,000 piloting trips.

Cockburn and his colleagues have absorbed Abbott's lessons, and simply extended them into another realm. The old ways of piloting, says Cockburn, are not just about good sea stories, they're all about good, proven practices that he and his modern colleagues supplement, with equally good technology. "As much as I love Billy Abbott," says Cockburn, "I wouldn't trade my computer for him, only because I think it does make the job safer, more efficient, you know. But having said that, piloting isn't about starting at a computer screen, either—the value of learning from somebody like Billy Abbott is that you're on the range he taught you on the Penobscot River, and then you look down at the computer, and the computer confirms the fact that you're just where you should be, and that's a great thing, to have two things saying the same thing." Abbott's stories, the routes he took from one point to another, says Cockburn, actually live in Cockburn's computer.

Piloting the IZ up the river to Bucksport starts this morning before Cockburn even gets on the ship. He has asked Hamilton to maneuver the pilot boat to give him a view of the ship's aft end: "I just want to make sure there's enough draft

Climbing aboard ship can be the riskiest part of a pilot's job.

back here to put a tugboat on the stern, which gives the best amount of leverage when handling the ship alongside the dock," says Cockburn, craning his neck to see the ship's stern. "So that's what we're taking a look at now, to see if we've got enough draft on the ship to put a tugboat right there, without getting underneath anything. Looks like we probably can." And then, with a smile, Cockburn says, "Time to head to the office!"

Hamilton pulls alongside the tanker. Water swishes and gurgles between the two vessels as he narrows the gap. A wood and rope ladder is lowered from the tanker's deck, thwacking against the ship's side. Cockburn, backpack hoisted onto his back, begins the climb up. He's greeted at the top by a contingent of crewmen, and led up the many flights to the bridge. As he climbs, he jokes that Stairmasters are part of a pilot's training regimen. A little winded, he walks confidently onto the bridge, extending his hand. "Good morning," he says to the captain. "Nice to see you, how are you?"

"Morning. You like drink?" This is the offer Cockburn has been waiting for. He

especially loves the cappucinos he gets on some of the more upscale ships. This morning, however, on this 17-year-old tanker with rust around the edges, he's aiming a little bit lower. "How about just some black coffee?"

And as a crewmember scurries off to get coffee, Cockburn brandishes his offerings to the captain, who has been at sea for six days since leaving Venezuela. "There's your newspaper, Captain," he says, "and this is for you too." It's a lottery ticket, geared to the season, which is Halloween. "You can win up to ten thousand dollars with this," says Cockburn, as everyone on the bridge laughs. "It's the 'Scream for Cash' and the rules are right there."

Jeff Cockburn is obviously comfortable being in charge; it's a prerequisite for being a ship's pilot. In high school, he was captain not only of the football team, but the basketball and baseball teams as well. But here's the paradox for ship's pilots: they have to be in charge aboard someone else's ship. It's their job to arrive on an unknown vessel and essentially tell the captain what to do, winning the captain's confidence and that of the crew loyal to him.

Ship piloting is a profession that goes back thousands of years, says Larry Wade, captain of the Maine Maritime Academy's training ship STATE OF MAINE who, prior to his stint at the Castine school, spent 30 years in the merchant marine, predominantly on tankers.

"It's an ancient profession that has evolved over the years from guys rowing out in a dory to meet a sailing ship coming up to the harbor, and whoever happened to get there first would lead the ship in. It evolved from that to the point where they actually boarded the ships and came into the ports, and then more recently they've changed so some of them are doing it by helicopter, landing on the ships and piloting them in.

"The reason for having a pilot," says Wade, "is you need the local knowledge and the pilot being home ported in that port has the local knowledge that a ship master who is travelling worldwide might not have of each port that you get to. He's there to advise the ship's master to keep him out of trouble."

Nowhere was piloting more necessary than along Maine's fogbound and rocky coast that bristled with ledges, rocks and shoals, and whose harbors were often at the far end of tricky river passages. As trade with the region grew in the 18th and 19th centuries, more and more ships arrived on the coast. And in the early days, piloting in Maine—and elsewhere—was a free-for-all. Pilots would dash out to a ship signaling them off the coast, often ignor-

Continued on page 94

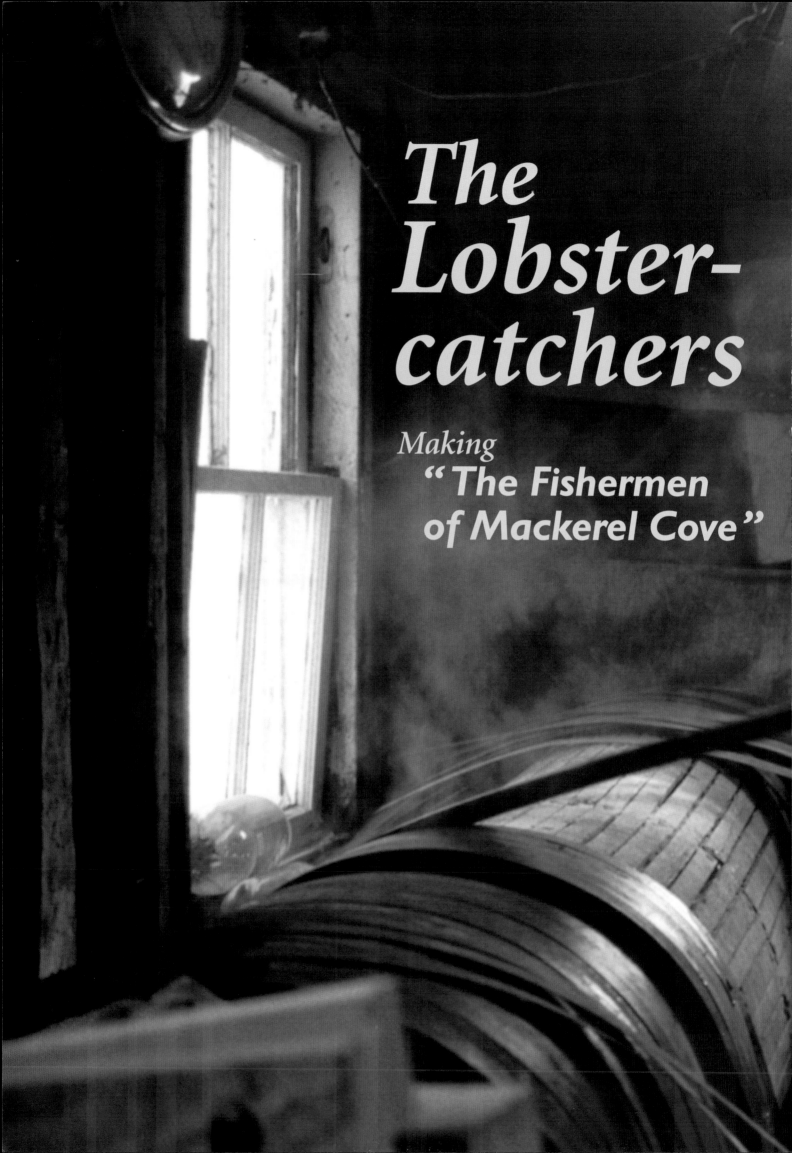

The Lobster-catchers

Making
**"The Fishermen
of Mackerel Cove"**

Story and photographs by
JOE GOLDMAN

February 1986

Every trip back became an arrival home, even the initial separation of three years since my first visit. I cannot account for the depth of feeling, based upon such a brief acquaintance with these people.

Bob Leeman greets me at his workshop door, "Been about a hundred years, hasn't it, Joe." He is building lobster traps, as all the fishermen do when the snow falls, and the seas are too rough for a boat to venture from the cove.

I make the rounds to their homes and fishhouses. Within hours, anyone passing through the General Store has heard of my return. We are soon conversing like I had been here only yesterday.

They share the news, of weather, threats to their livelihood, of the hindrances of old age, family relations and the prospects for lobstering.

Rip Black (above) won an Olympic medal in 1928, and is a college graduate. Jesse Johnson (below) is a farmer as well, with a pasture by the sea. Their history encompasses all kinds of fishing, from the Grand Banks searching for cod, handlining from dories, to catching swordfish by harpoon, to sardining with seines in the quiet night.

"The ocean is a big place, but it seems to be getting smaller and smaller." Marty has a tone of frustration and bitterness. "A fisherman can't afford to switch gear for a different catch like years ago, too many big outfits; factory ships trawl entire schools of fish."

But Marty is an "off-islander". He came from Small Point, within sight of Bailey Island. He moved here because you can gauge the weather better on this side of the bay. However, after 40 years, he is still considered an outsider by those born here.

In my observation of others, I would learn about myself. They prefer a separateness from the rest of the world. Later I will wonder, how much I have changed due to my growing friendships with these people; and how much like them I may have been to begin with.

Ornery, private, yet receptive to my interest. I made clear I was not here under any sponsorship as a reporter or an employee. My occupation as a craftsman, a theatrical stagehand in New York City, encouraged their trust.

The islanders who attracted my attention the most were Rip Black and Jesse Johnson, still active lobstermen, well into their 80s.

They lived next door to one another, atop a ridge which runs across the middle of the island. They had grown up together, worked as teenagers and young men aboard Rip's father's schooner. They had done all types of fishing. And Rip had graduated college in the 1920s. He had won a bronze medal in the 1928 Olympics in Amsterdam, for the hammer throw.

He and Jesse are "kingpins" on the island. These elderly seafarers, held in esteem not only by the fishermen of Mackerel Cove; their renown extends up and down the Maine coast.

Both are imposing figures, athletic in build; educated and quick. Besides lobstering, they have spent decades hooktrawling, handlining, harpooning swordfish, mackerel-pounding, tuna-fishing, gill-netting, sardining and dragging for shrimp. They spent autumns up-country, deer hunting, and winters duck hunting.

Rip had been Selectman for the township. Jesse kept up a lifelong correspondence with naturalists and visitors who had frequented the island.

Both had a choice of other careers. Jobs ashore would have been more profitable, more secure, and with less physical risk. But they chose to continue as fishermen.

They love work, as they love the sea, and are willing to face death with dignity.

My search took on a life of its own. What began as a simple documentary exercise would become a complex journey; a personal odyssey.

I wanted to become part of this island, to be from here, and to find a way to adopt their past as my own. It seemed a vital connection to my image of our nation. The integrity these people demonstrated, their approach to work, their honest appraisal of life. Their character seemed to resonate with a national persona.

They aspire to a mythical self-image; the embodiment of ideals that underlie a spirit that holds continuity with the past. They trace their ancestry to the first colonial settlers of the early 1700s. For nearly 300 years, while others moved westward, these folks have remained.

What would unfold over the years of my journey was a growing relationship with these men, my acceptance into an insular society and an understanding that their "pastoral" existence was not without conflict, great hardships and loneliness.

But there was an inner drive they all possessed. They had little need for decorative trimmings, nor any interest in amassing wealth or fame. They relish life and the sense of renewal, they are consummate naturalists, and admire self-reliance.

While the documentary film would refrain from probing matters that were overly personal, when out of range of the tape recorder and camera, they would confide in me. As I would in them.

At 80, Rip Black still engages in a contest with the sea.

The secrecy surrounding their craft and their community would gradually be penetrated.

It turns out that their trade is an art. But it would be difficult for people not prone to speak of feelings to relate these to a stranger. Methods of their craft, practiced intuitively, they had learned with a sixth sense, while growing up. How would I address this using words?

"A lobsterman won't tell you where he set his traps. In summertime they set in shoal water. Then there are times when people steal lobsters, but more often than not people have been accused who never had nothin' to do with it."

Bob Leeman left to serve 20 years as chief petty officer aboard U.S. Navy nuclear submarines. Yet no matter how long a career he had off the island, he returned as if it had been merely a brief diversion from his true calling as fisherman, always at the border of land's end.

To translate this onto film; to find the significance, emphasis, and context of what I saw and photographed intermittently would be my challenge. And how would I discover things in my own experience and transpose those revelations in a documentary?

Off the beaten path, they lived in a place that was bleak and barren, their muted surroundings, often colored by nostalgia.

"Seasons pass so quickly when you're near the end." Rip sits in his kitchen, reflecting upon what had been "before the bridge." He recalls being off Georges Bank, for five weeks at a stretch, until the ice ran out for keeping the cod, mackerel or swordfish they had caught.

They would speak of stacking dories or mending nets ashore. Of waiting for the steam packet, bringing mail, supplies and summer tourists down to Steamboat Wharf. There were music and dances, cribbage nights and potluck suppers.

Today, when the fog rolls in to envelop the island, all attachments to an outside world disappear. It's like stepping into a time machine. Seated among the old men in Clayte's fish house near Bass Rock, hearing tales of their Acadian past; or walking across the snow-covered fields of Jesse's pasture by the sea.

But these old men were not sedentary. Rip was the first out of the cove on mornings at 4 A.M., hauling his traps by hand from an open

Jesse, 83, feeding the lambs.

skiff even in rough stormy weather, backside of the island, near Giant Stairs and Thunderhole.

Their work takes on a depth of meaning, seasoned by a lifetime of activity, and an undiminished fascination with nature.

"No one would understand it without knowing the ocean. I always wanted the open spaces and the sea, never any question, I always knew I'd be a fisherman."

There is such inner conviction, certainty and self-assertion, in the midst of a stark and Spartan existence; hovering under the unpredictable, ever-ruling forces of sea and sky.

Jesse used to raise horses and cattle on his saltwater farm, in addition to his fishing full-time. They live for their work. Even in his 80s, he still herds a flock of sheep, tending to the birth of the lambs in February and March. I would sit with him in his "pine room" while he carved decoys. "Years ago, you had no choice but to survive off of nature." And Jesse would speak on, thoughts he had saved up a lifetime, and I felt blessed to hear a man's story. Jesse's spot became the center of the universe.

How would I capture this place? How would I do justice to relating feelings about this life? There were periods when I felt suspended in twilight.

…we hear of their frustrations, doubts, and the paradox of the sea being the source of both their anger and their passion. Steve (above) is confronted with the possibility of giving up his boat.

The summer cottages lay boarded up. The blizzard kept on. A harsh wind swept the snow horizontally across the landscape.

Their fatalism is matter of fact. "If I make it this March, I'll set traps again," Rip comments. "Drowning is not a bad way to go, at least they don't have to go to the trouble of burying you or scattering your ashes... wouldn't mind being buried at the entrance of the cove, 'cause I always feel so good when I come round the point."

George relates his father's last moments, "The day before he died, he looked up at his wife, clear as a bell and says, 'darn it, I don't wanna die, but I know that I gotta, and I guess I may as well sooner than later.'"

They shape their destiny as best they are able. "I don't know what it is, but living by the sea, something gets in your blood. You might have noticed we're pretty independent here. I mean I respect the law, to an extent. But there's a point where even the law plays too much. Tries to play too much a part of telling you what to do."

If I thought this would simply be a trip to Brigadoon, I was wrong. There were complex relationships. And how do you get close without offending? There would be friends who grew apart, marriages that failed, deaths in the family, along with the vicissitudes of the fish industry. There were disputes over property, over fishing territory and scores to be settled.

I would learn the difficulties Steve has in keeping his own boat, and of working as a sternman. The restlessness that makes for "cabin fever." The question of whether Jesse's grandson Kenny will be able to learn the family trade and be accepted by the other Bailey Island fishermen. Will Dave work in the nearby shipyard, the Bath Iron Works, and be forced to give up lobstering to support his family through the winter? Will realtors buy up key land around the cove, interfering with the fisherman's right of way? Has technology and the corporate economy destroyed the fisherman's independence? Would competition drive even the most dedicated out of business?

Is America's legacy of freedom fading? Who will pass on the torch?

It would be my task to grasp what is essential, and not sacrifice their privacy or our friendships. To anticipate, just as they intuit the weather, and navigate with dead-reckoning; just as they respond to the meandering of nature, I too would learn to navigate my way.

I was offered a passport into their lives. I experienced a rite of passage. My life ultimately became entwined with theirs; their communal past, an extension of my own.

In the course of my journals, I would re-examine the kernel of my experience. I was usually trying to catch up with their activity, never in front of it. I always felt as if I was lagging behind, just missing something important. What is at the root of human experience, and how do I transpose the subtle and elusive qualities of life?

All my days spent aboard their boats, out in the cold. And inside their shops, at the supper table and mornings at the General Store, seated round the stove. It was not a matter of becoming invisible; with my lights and cameras this was impossible. But in letting go of preconceived ideas and pretence, I could accept others as they are. And for me, it was a long lesson in growing up.

I had to learn patience, to see how they see. Frequently, the most significant occurrences are hidden in the unseen. I would create a film from glimpses, like the assembly of pieces to a jigsaw puzzle.

The style of which would be in keeping with their cadence, their riddles and speech. The rhythm of their movements timed with the rhythm of the sea. And each person would represent a facet of a unified mosaic, interconnected like the elements of nature.

Their character became defined by word and deed. And I would try to walk in their shoes. Rip would tell me, "Living in an age when everyone was family. You walked in the door around suppertime, and you were asked to be seated, and you ate dinner and left through the other door. It was like that, casual all the time, and you could lie awake at night and think of everyone on the island and know everything about them."

And I discovered I was entering their stage. Walking the paths of their past as well as the present.

The experience which most distilled my feelings for the odyssey took place one midnight, in the heart of winter. In the eye of a passing blizzard, when the night sky cleared to reveal a full dome of stars.

Jesse Johnson and I headed down to the barn, where one of the ewes was expected to give birth soon. It seemed above that the whole galaxy was visible. The air was crisp, and our boots crunched through the hard top layer of thick snow. Below where the field sloped gently down to meet the sea, we could hear the surf crash and tumble by the water's edge.

Jesse was sharing this gift of life; opening a window to his soul, showing me what had made him happy and strong. I felt honored and grateful for our walk through the snow, over the island hill; from that point and moment we shared in time and space, and with the breath I inhaled, I became born of this island, the center of the universe; aloft in time, with all history and the future extending around me.

---

*New York filmmaker **Joe Goldman** has crafted "The Fishermen of Mackerel Cove" as a feature-length documentary motion picture.*

Clayle Johnson

Rip Black

Dewey Greeley

A PERSONAL JOURNEY
The Fishermen of Mackerel Cove

Joe Goldman shot footage on Bailey Island during a dozen visits to the community between 1983 and 1993. During the same time period he also took more than 1,200 still photographs depicting his subjects and their lives.

BROTHERS

ON THE ROCK

WITH TIME OUT FOR WAR AND A LONG WALK, DOUG AND HARRY ODOM HAVE DEVOTED SEVEN DECADES TO ONE MAINE ISLAND

COLIN WOODARD

With their older brother, the Odoms arrived on Monhegan in 1930.

In 1930, at the start of the Great Depression, Doug and Harry Odom got their first look at Monhegan Island. Their older brother Sidney, 22, had been dispatched by his boss to run the island's little summer store and he took Doug and Harry, 16 and 14, up from Quincy, Massachusetts to help him.

"I took one look at it and said, 'What the hell am I doing on a rock like this?'" Harry recalls. "I told my brother I wasn't impressed at all. But when the fall came, I hated going in! As a kid, to take trips and walk all over that island. Oh, it was a great place." The boys couldn't wait to come back.

Sidney's company called him ashore seven years later, but Doug and Harry would spend most of their lives on Monhegan. They purchased the island store and over more than three decades built it into a year-round operation and one of the hubs of island life. They engaged in winter fishing, and were still out in January, hauling lobster traps together in 1994, when Harry was 78 and Doug 80. Over the decades they cut ice, delivered fuel and groceries, served in town government. Last year they moved inshore for the winter for the first time since 1945, to be closer to health and public services.

The Odom Brothers © Jamie Wyeth, 2001

When the Odoms first came out, there were four Model T Ford trucks and three crank telephones on the island. Their store had one of each, along with a small Delco 32-volt generator and a bank of batteries that powered the lights and a tiny freezer. Everything else in the store was refrigerated with blocks of ice cut from the ice pond up on the hill behind the lighthouse. Sidney, Doug and Harry ran a full-service operation, delivering groceries directly to customers' homes, which in those days included large summer households whose wealthy owners maintained full staffs of black household servants. At such households, grocery deliveries and those who delivered them were only welcome at the back door or servants' entrances.

"People on Monhegan were very friendly, even with all the strangers," Harry recalls. And with all the out-of-state summer folks around, he noticed that island children didn't have a real Maine accent like their peers in communities inshore.

Throughout the 1930s, the store remained a seasonal operation. Come winter, Harry went inshore to work as a salesman for the Rockland office of the John Bird grocery chain, while Doug was employed by the Kennedy Butter and Egg Stores in Massachusetts. (Doug and Harry ultimately purchased the store, while their older brother resumed his full-time job on the mainland.) But Doug and Harry would return for a few weeks every winter to cut ice, ensuring another summer of refrigerated meats and groceries at the store, chilled fish in boats' holds and iced drinks at summer hotels and cocktail parties.

Indeed, until gas refrigeration became affordable in the late 1950s, the entire male population of the island turned out each year to cut, carry and store nearly 300 tons of ice. In the 19th century, ice was one of Maine's most important exports; cold winters and an ample supply from unpolluted lakes and ponds made Maine the source for much of the refrigeration used in the teeming cities of the Eastern seaboard. Because of the island's isolation, Monhegan's ice cutting industry survived into the early 1970s, and the Odom store had an ice delivery business on the side. In winter, Doug often operated the gasoline-powered "groover" which cut a checkerboard of grooves into the surface of the pond. One-hundred-fifty pound blocks of ice would be broken out using saws and splitting bars, then stored between layers of sawdust in the island ice house. The Odoms were the main consumers of island ice, which reduced their reliance on expensive, temperamental generators.

As the clouds of war gathered, Doug took full-time work operating cranes at the

Fifty years after the fact, courtesy of Sen. Olympia Snowe, Harry Odom gets his World War II medals;

naval shipyard back in Quincy, while Harry tended the store. But within two years the brothers were 12,000 miles apart, fighting in battles on opposite ends of the planet.

Doug served in the engine room of the USS MASSACHUSETTS, a 35,000-ton battleship he'd watched being built while he was perched atop a shipyard crane. The MASSACHUSETTS was a fortunate ship. Doug recalls there being not a single combat death among the ship's crew of 2,500, despite taking two shell hits during a naval battle outside German-occupied Casablanca and three years spent in the Central Pacific providing support to amphibious landings against the Japanese. Doug was aboard the MASSACHUSETTS for more than three years, returning to Quincy after the Japanese surrender.

Harry was drafted into the Army, a staff sergeant in a unit that engaged in heavy fighting in Sicily and northern France. He was wounded by shrapnel shortly after the Normandy landings and spent two weeks in an English hospital; he returned to find that many of his buddies had been killed. Shortly thereafter, while occupying a knoll on the front, Germans overran his position. Harry was captured and shipped to a prisoner of war camp in German-occupied Poland where he spent the next six or seven months surviving on meager rations: a bowl of potato soup and a piece of bread once a day.

"They didn't abuse me but it was really rough not having enough to eat," he recalls. "I used to be a chow hound and boy, did that hit me hard."

Then in February 1945, Harry heard the thunder of Russian artillery slowly advancing from the east. Soon the shells were falling on Germans and Allied pris-

Over the past two decades, Doug and Harry have sold property to young fishing families for a fraction of what the market could have borne

oners alike. Amidst the mayhem and retreating Germans, Harry and a small group of fellow POWs took off, walking eastward across Poland and Russia. They hitched rides on passing cars and freight trains, even rode bicycles for a bit, but mostly they walked. They spent nights in abandoned homes or were taken in and fed by Polish or Russian civilians in the dozens of towns they passed through. In the end Harry and his companions made their way to one of Russia's Black Sea ports and were invited aboard an Australian freighter bound for Egypt. There they found a British ship that took them back to American-occupied Naples. The Army promptly shipped the former prisoners home, and Harry arrived in Quincy in April, two months after fleeing the German camp and four months before the end of the war. (Escaped prisoners of war weren't allowed to return to their units and would be shot if recaptured by the enemy.)

"I'd been sleeping on the ground, in box cars, on hard floors," recalls Harry, who received four medals including a Purple Heart. "When I got back to my mother's she said, 'oh, you sleep in here,' a room with a bed with all those soft, thick mattresses. I couldn't sleep in it. I took a pillow and laid on the floor."

But while Doug and Harry were off fighting the war, the store had gone into debt. "They thought they'd run the store and get out of debt and then go their separate ways on the mainland," their nephew Ben Odom says. "But by the time they got out of debt they were sort of captured by the island."

Black Star photographer Kosti Ruohomaa shot the Odoms aboard their boat in the 1950s.

They had also started building what Harry calls "the finest island store on the coast of Maine," with a year-around operation with a walk-in cooler, butcher counter and a remarkable array of luxury items. Monhegan hadn't had a store like this before, and hasn't since it closed more than a decade ago.

"It would be nothing to have whole steer legs of beef, or a pig or sheep hanging up in the cooler because Doug had learned to be a butcher when he worked for Kennedy Eggs," recalls Ben Odom, who worked in the store each summer for

a decade. "Since Harry had worked for a wholesale grocer he knew where to get unusual products." Every year they'd have 30 or 40 wheels of aged cheese from Vermont and a half dozen bottles of wine that cost $100 each. "Yachtsmen would make a special trip to get them."

But Doug and Harry had another pursuit in winter: lobstering. They'd started fishing in dories, hauling lobster traps or tub trawling for halibut. In 1946 they bought their first lobsterboat, the JULIET H, and began fishing together. They would continue to do so for another half

Over the years the Odoms built what Harry calls "the best island store on the coast of Maine."

century. Their third boat, CHRIS, a wooden 30-footer, is still fishing out of Monhegan's exposed harbor.

But disaster struck in November 1963. One of the store's generators backfired, setting a grass fire that spread into the oil and bottled gas storage area. Exploding gas and 45-knot winds spread burning oil onto surrounding buildings. Doug and Harry had been building traps in the store when the fire started, and had nearly put out the fire when the well they were using ran dry. Town water had been shut off for the winter and hoses thrown in the sea became clogged with seaweed thrown up by the passing storm. "For a while it was feared the island would have to be evacuated," island resident Alta Ashley wrote at the time. Eight buildings were lost in the fire, including the store and Doug and Harry's home. "This island has been as if without a heart since the fire," Ashley wrote.

When word got around that Doug and Harry were underinsured and might not be able to rebuild, some summer residents intervened with private loans. By late January the Odoms were rebuilding both home and store and in spring the present Monhegan Store building was open for business. The brothers ran a successful store there for another decade and a half, but subsequent owners weren't as able. At this writing, the Monhegan Store building has been standing vacant and empty for years.

By the turn of the century, Doug and Harry had an inseparable companion: a diligently loyal Jack Russell named Taxi. The dog was a gift of dog breeder (and sometime painter) Jamie Wyeth, who on extremely short notice announced the tiny dog would be arriving on the island by helicopter. Today Taxi screens visitors, licking those he approves of and cornering suspect persons with determined barking.

Today most islanders agree that the main threat to Monhegan's year-around community is the explosive growth in island property values. With modest seasonal cottages selling for half a million dollars, young fishermen find it difficult to purchase—or even rent—year-around accommodations. But over the past two decades, Doug and Harry have sold property to young fishing families for a fraction of what the market could have borne.

"I think Doug and Harry feel strongly that the island would be a different place without fishing families," says Tralice Bracy, whose husband, Robert, lobsters from Monhegan. The Bracys' new home stands on a lot sold to them by the Odoms at great discount. "If you're starting out as a young fisherman, you already have a huge investment in your boat and traps; and if you're investing in property as well, it's definitely a hard go. This was a huge gift for us from Doug and Harry and their family as well."

"We look at Boothbay as a good example of a place that's full of new people who own all the good spots and all that," Harry says. "If you took these lots that we sold to [fishermen] and you had all summer people there, then there'd be nobody to take care of the island in wintertime. That would be a mess."

Harry Odom says Monhegan's unique community will persevere. With two-thirds of the island in the hands of the Monhegan Associates land trust and protected in its natural state, and a community of committed winter fishermen, Harry expects Monhegan's unique community will continue to persevere. "Fifty years from now," he says, "I don't think it will have changed too much. It's nice to have it that way."

Colin Woodard is author of Ocean's End: Travels Through Endangered Seas. *Taxi, for reasons that are unclear, approves of him. Family photographs courtesy of* **Ben Odom**.

BARTLETT'S ISLAND, 1945

Kosti Ruohomaa photographs a weekend with Phillips H. Lord

DEANNA BONNER-GANTER

Radio producer Phillips Haynes Lord purchased 3,000-acre Bartlett's Island off Mount Desert in 1939. He was 42 at the time. Lord's parents were natives of Ellsworth; as a boy he had summered in Sedgwick. At the peak of his radio celebrity, Lord made Bartlett's a refuge from the pressures of his career in New York City.

Kosti Ruohomaa, a photographer with New York-based Black Star Publishing Co., was in Rockland in August 1945, for the blueberry harvest. In what was most likely a self-assignment, he arranged to spend a weekend on Bartlett's with Lord, his family and friends. While there, he shot the photographs on the following pages. The pictures remained in Ruohomaa's files and have never been published as a complete piece.

As a radio producer, Lord would base a script on real-life experiences and factual material. "We the People," begun 1936 and running until 1951, contained a human-interest mix of unknowns telling their own sometimes bizarre stories. "Seth Parker," a character Lord had created in 1928, was based on a Down East preacher's weekly living room reception for the locals to pray, tell stories and sing hymns. NBC broadcast the program to a nationwide audience as "Sunday Evening at Seth Parker's." Phillips played Seth Parker himself.

At the time Ruohomaa shot these pictures, Lord was actively writing "Gangbusters." Recalled as a noisy, action-packed show, it was based on true stories taken from J. Edgar Hoover's FBI "dead" files. "Gangbusters" had a run of 12 years.

Dr. Albert J. Lord reads a script as son Phillips listens respectfully. Dr. Lord was an alumnus of Bowdoin College, as was his son, who graduated in 1923. Kosti Ruohomaa from Black Star © Time Inc. Picture Collection.

Facing Page: "B.I." a four-year-old colt born and raised on Bartlett's Island (and whose initials stand for Bartlett's Island) pulls Phillips Lord and his wife, Donnie, on a surrey ride. Kosti Ruohomaa from Black Star © Time Inc. Picture Collection.

Evening by lamplight in the spacious living room of the main house. Left to right: Shirley Kerr of New York, Lord's secretary who oversaw his New York office; Donnie Boone Lord. Phillips Lord, seated in rattan chair, looks on; Mary Elizabeth Stevens Bobst in the foreground. Kosti Ruohomaa from Black Star (3) © Time Inc. Picture Collection.

In 1941 Lord married Donnie Eugena Boone (a direct descendent of Daniel Boone, noted Ruohomaa in his notes), who appears in these photographs.

During his 16-year ownership of Bartlett's, Lord revived farming, husbandry, weir-fishing and boatbuilding. He maintained an active sawmill, shingle mill and a blacksmith's forge. Hay was grown and cut for winter storage. He kept a few riding horses, cows, pigs, hens, turkeys and about 300 sheep. Three fish weirs yielded regular catches of herring. Clams were harvested with a hose-watering method Lord devised himself. Canned "Seth Parker Clam Chowder" became well known for a time.

Lord sold off his programs and production company in 1953. In 1955 he sold Bartlett's to Mr. and Mrs. David Rockefeller.

Ruohomaa's photographs from sometimes-unusual vantage points express a subjective vision uncommon in 1940s magazine work. They reflect Ruohomaa's familiarity with the Hollywood studio environment where he had previously worked. There's an aura to the Bartlett's Island scenes suggesting stills from a film. Composition, lighting and location factor into the action, with views of the island and awareness of distant Cadillac Mountain.

In 1945 Ruohomaa was only one year into his contract with the Black Star agency, but his photographs had already appeared on a LIFE magazine cover (May 1, 1944) and in numerous features. His nine-page essay, "Maine Winter," appeared in February 1945, and included poetry specially composed for it by Bowdoin College professor Robert P. Tristram Coffin.

Ruohomaa was born in Quincy, Massachusetts, and was brought to Maine by his Finnish parents when he was almost 13. The family homestead and blueberry farm overlooked Penobscot Bay from Dodge's Mountain, Rockland. He graduated from Rockland High School, where he acquired a lifelong love of poetry and literature and was urged to study art. Spotted by a Walt Disney talent scout after studying commercial art in Boston, he spent five years as an assistant in effects animation at Walt Disney Studios.

A portfolio of Gallup, New Mexico, Native American Indian portraits and hobo life in Santa Barbara won him the contract with Black Star in 1944. Through Black Star, Ruohomaa's photography was distributed nationally and abroad to major weekly and monthly publications. His black-and-white photographs were recognized in photography journals.

Ruohomaa's photographic interest narrowed to documenting the character of New England life, particularly Maine. Hard work close to the land and sea, the habits, expressions and humor of New England people, and themes of winter became his preoccupations.

Deanna Bonner-Ganter *is Curator of Photography, Art and Archives at the Maine State Museum. She is completing a monograph of the life and photography of Kosti Ruohomaa.*

Phillips Lord plays the organ as "Pipsqueak," his pet fawn, gets curious.

Two young bulls demonstrate stubborn reluctance after a voyage from the mainland. The moment seems curiously orchestrated. Kosti Ruohomaa from Black Star (2) © Neelo Lofman Estate Collection

Ruohomaa, atop the towboat cabin, photographs the barge transport across Bartlett Narrows from Mount Desert to Bartlett's Island.

Phillips Lord would catch 700 to 800 bushels of herring in his weir in an ordinary season— "but it's the chance of a really big catch which keeps him and every weir-fisherman going," noted Ruohomaa's caption of this scene. Kosti Ruohomaa from Black Star (2) © Neelo Lofman Estate Collection

Ruohomaa had lots of experience photographing beautiful models and actresses during his five years in Hollywood.

Preparing home-made clam chowder produced and canned under the label "Seth Parker" and sold in limited quantities to an exclusive clientele, including New York's Waldorf Astoria Hotel. Using clams dug from Bartlett's Island's beaches, "no expense was spared to make this the finest clam chowder," noted Ruohomaa.

Mix

PORTLAND STRUGGLES TO UNDERSTAND ITS WATERFRONT

Story by
JOAN AMORY

Photographs by
CHRISTOPHER AYRES

"Look out this window," exclaims Capt. Jeff Monroe as he gestures to the west. "That's a beautiful sight, a working waterfront: the fishing fleet, the International Marine Terminal, boat repair—there are more different kinds of things going on here than meet the eye!"

Monroe, Portland's Director of Transportation, makes his case: a working waterfront must be diverse to be healthy. From his office in Portland's Marine Trade Center, he looks out at the new container cargo crane looming over the International Marine Terminal. Rows of orange Hapag-Lloyd containers wait in the parking lot to be loaded for shipment to Halifax and the world beyond.

Portland, this venerable East Coast port, is now the second largest oil port in "through port" tonnage on the Atlantic Coast—behind only New York City. And it ranks first in New England for overall gross "through" tonnage.

Surprising? You bet. Oil accounts for 90 percent of Portland's tonnage, with much less dry cargo. Close to 35 million tons of cargo of all kinds moved through the harbor in 2001, on over 700 ships. And Portland and Boston switch back and forth claiming to have the most international passengers arriving in New England by sea.

But let's not be picky about the statistics. The fact remains that over the last 25 years, over fits and starts, Portland's waterfront has again become an economic workhorse for the city, the state, New England and the northwest Atlantic.

![Tiny's Fish Market storefront with signs reading SCALLOP, HADDOCK, SOLE, STEAMERS, LOBSTERS, SHRIMP 1 29, S. MEAT 4 9, TINY'S FISH MARKET, LIVE LOBSTER, TO TRAVEL WE SHIP](img)

Traditional uses must be part of Portland harbor's future.

The port is now faced with a happy problem: how to develop 17 acres of prime land at the east end of Portland's waterfront that Bath Iron Works has transferred to the city. But first, to put matters in context, let's look back at what has worked on the waterfront in past years.

The port's current success is in stark contrast to years of decline that began well before World War I. World War II brought a burst of activity as the North Atlantic fleet used the harbor as its home port and 266 Liberty ships were launched from South Portland's shipyards. In the late 1940s, during the days of the Marshall Plan, more grain passed through Portland headed for Europe than any other port. These spurts were, however, only temporary. The grain silos closed for good in the early 1960s. (Today their great hewn beams, some 14 by 18 inches, can be seen in Rockland's Samoset Hotel.) After World War II transportation found new routes on Interstate highways and, except for oil, Portland harbor was left behind.

Recent changes have been concentrated in the 2,500-yard section of Commercial Street east of the new Casco Bay Bridge. This stretch of shoreline is a jigsaw puzzle of public and private property, with maintained and decaying wharves, parking lots, marine contractors, ferry terminals, condos, navy and coast guard facilities, fish processing, lobster boats, draggers, tugs, restaurants and pleasure boats. It's what city planner Alan Holt calls "a messy mix," like life itself.

The Portland Fish Exchange uses an innovative daily auction to attract buyers.

PUBLIC, PRIVATE AND IN BETWEEN

The waterfront's gradual resurgence came from a variety of initiatives, often through public-private partnerships. In the 1970s the city built the International Marine Terminal on the site of an old railroad terminal that had reverted to the city for unpaid taxes. The business community chipped in, helping to raise the necessary funds to build the new facility. For over 30 years the SCOTIA PRINCE has sailed daily between Portland and Yarmouth, Nova Scotia, carrying passengers, cars and trucks during a six-month season.

In the early 1980s Gov. Joseph E. Brennan and the city used tax incentives and state bond money to lure Bath Iron Works into locating a new ship repair facility and floating drydock at Maine State Pier, on the east end of Commercial Street. Portland's offer beat out Boston, and for 20 years BIW used the facility to finish out and repair Navy cruisers, destroyers and frigates. In 1986 a new ferry terminal serving the Casco Bay island communities opened on the west side of the pier, again using state bond financing.

The Portland Fish Exchange was founded in 1986 by a coalition of fish processors, fishing vessel owners and the city's Economic Development Authority. The exchange uses an innovative daily auction to attract buyers, improve prices paid to fishermen and reward fishermen who improve the quality of their catch. Before the auction, fishermen sold to whomever showed up at the wharf where their boats tied up; they now have direct access to a competitive market through the exchange. The Fish Pier, constructed though bond financing, services 300 vessels and has landings of between 20 and 30 million pounds.

The Fish Exchange changed the location of fish processing, long a mainstay of the waterfront. Before the auction, fish were off-loaded directly from a boat to the fish processor. Now fish move from boats to the auction, and then are loaded on a truck. Trucks can take the fish anywhere for processing—to one of three processing facilities on the Fish Pier, to new processing facilities near the interstate, or to older plants on wharves farther down Commercial Street.

Jack Humeniuk, the leader of Portland's longshoremen, worked with other harbor leaders to bring a container facility to the waterfront. In 1989 their efforts resulted in a bond issue that financed a 350-foot extension of the International Marine Terminal. In 1991 Hapag-Lloyd began its container feeder service, shipping containers to Halifax for transshipment. Since then the SCOTIA PRINCE passenger ferry and its passengers have shared the terminal with container ships, trucks and containers. With container shipments showing double-digit growth every year until 2000, each square foot of space at the terminal is used.

In 1977, restaurateur Tony DiMillo bought Long Wharf and developed a marina. He moved his eatery from the upland side of Commercial Street to a renovated ferryboat next to his marina. His floating

restaurant and marina were welcomed by the city. However, on either side of DiMillo, on Central Wharf and Portland Pier, condominium development in the mid-1980s brought out strong public opposition. In 1983 Paul E. Merrill, owner of a successful trucking company, opened a bulk cargo operation on the inner harbor at the far west end of Commercial Street. It met opposition from an adjacent upscale residential neighborhood because of noise, but then successfully cohabited with its neighbors under a noise ordinance adopted by the City.

Oil imports, the mainstay of the port, are located on the South Portland side of the harbor on either side of the Casco Bay Bridge. Made possible by a wartime pipeline built in 1941 from South Portland to Montreal, the pipeline makes use of Portland's ice-free port to provide crude oil to eastern Canada. In 1999 a new pipeline was constructed along the same route. Oil imports have nearly doubled in the past two years, reaching over 180 million barrels.

The construction of the Casco Bay Bridge (1998) over the harbor and dredging the main harbor channel (1998-99) made navigating in the harbor safer. The bridge's increased vertical clearance and a wider opening made it easier for ships to access the inner harbor west of the bridge.

The city has courted cruise ships over the past decade. In 2001 45 cruise ships visited Portland, up from 22 in 1998. Some dock at the International Marine Terminal and some at the Maine State Pier, while others anchor offshore and ferry in their passengers when both piers are occupied. The state is exploring high-speed ferries connecting Portland to Boston and Down East Maine. Planners suggest that Portland's future lies in attracting cruise ships and serving as an intermodal hub for travelers on high-speed ferries and passenger trains.

What's next? Right now, Portland owns more than 17 acres of prime land and two piers on the eastern end of Commercial Street. Much of the adjacent private property, once the railroad yards for Grand Trunk Railroad, is available for development. Lumped together, the city has a historic opportunity to shape the waterfront for years to come.

The land's availability coincides with city plans for the harbor developed after two decades of studies and reports. The studies recommend consolidating all ferry and cruise passenger ships on the eastern end of the waterfront, next to the retail section of Commercial Street. Container cargo would remain at the International Marine Terminal on the western end. Heavier marine industries would remain

The JULIE N oil spill was a lesson in the fragility of the harbor's marine environment.

clustered nearby on the west side of the waterfront. Traffic patterns would be redirected: passengers and freight for the international ferry would use the Franklin Arterial, at the east end of the waterfront, to connect to I-295. Truck traffic serving the International Marine Terminal, Fish Pier and industrial facilities would access I-295 via a new connector (slated for construction in 2003) paralleling west Commercial Street. Traffic in Commercial Street's congested center zone would be reduced.

DEBATE

There's a fierce debate over what should be done with the BIW lands. The various groups weighing in reflect the battles of the last 20 years that have shaped the current waterfront.

Many Portland citizens hold a bedrock belief that their working waterfront is vital to the city's history and identity. Aroused in the late 1980s by condominiums built on Chandler's Wharf (previously one of the largest working fishing piers) and angered by the prospect of more condos taking over the working waterfront, Portland activists formed a Waterfront Alliance. They sponsored a 1987 referendum that restricted zoning on the waterfront side of Commercial Street to "maritime uses" only.

"Working waterfront" is a nebulous concept. Some would define it a place where fishermen are able to tie up their boats, unload their catches, and mend their nets on piers and wharves at any time of day. Others would broaden the definition to include light manufacturing, boat repair or even certain types of office work and commercial activity. Many simply want to see fishermen and fishing boats as part of their daily lives, and they want the hustle and bustle of ships, tugs, ferries and barges, and the (sometimes inconvenient) drama of drawbridge openings for stately tankers.

There's also a strong sense that out-of-state developers shouldn't be able to lock up a piece of the waterfront and prevent public access. Condo dwellers, it was feared, would complain about smelly fish and engines gunned in the early morning hours, and try and force fishermen to change their uncouth ways.

It helps to remember what a deepwater shoreline offers: a place where land and sea interface, a place of exchange. A working waterfront is part of a transportation chain, and it must have infrastructure: tugs, pilots, chandleries, repair facilities, land-side transportation. That infrastructure requires a lot of investment. Marine businesses and fishermen typically can't afford substantial rents or wharfage. Wharf owners have historically rented a portion of their space to higher-rent commercial tenants to increase revenue. They were deprived of that source of income by the 1987 referendum, and wharf owners found it difficult to replace pilings, dredge slips and take the mundane but essential steps needed to maintain their wharves. Each piling costs around $1,000 to replace. Dredging, after an arduous permit process that can take up to 15 years, is

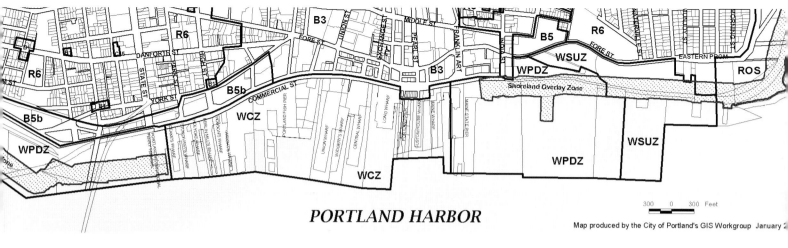

PORTLAND HARBOR

Map produced by the City of Portland's GIS Workgroup January 2

very costly, particularly when one adds in $15 per cubic yard for nearby disposal or $150 per cubic yard for upland disposal of contaminated spoils.

Virtually no waterfront development occurred in the years following the referendum. Longtime tenants left for upland sites. Leavitt and Parris, for example, formerly sailmakers, had switched to tent and awning production when sail power declined. After years of providing ice to fish packers and loading coal from trains, Elm Ice and Oil had turned to residential oil delivery. The referendum pushed both companies to move off the waterfront to locations more easily reached by car and truck. The Harris Company, an industrial supply concern, moved to an upland site rather than expand its waterfront location. None of these companies could be replaced by other non-maritime businesses. The deep recession of the late 1980s and early 90s made it more difficult for wharf owners to invest in infrastructure, even without the referendum's strictures. The referendum made the problem worse.

The referendum's impact on waterfront development and infrastructure had the subtlety of a sledge hammer, but it certainly focused public attention on the waterfront. The zoning freeze gave Portland breathing room, time to consider what a working waterfront is and evaluate other trends changing the waterfront. The Waterfront Alliance evolved from a single-issue (anti-condominium) citizen group to a comprehensive coalition representing diverse waterfront interests. Meeting monthly, it became an important presence in Portland's waterfront planning.

The 1987 referendum had a sunset provision that terminated its freeze in 1993. In the early 1990s, the Waterfront Alliance spent two years developing a proposal for revised waterfront zoning, finally

sending it to the city council. The proposal would have permitted a substantial expansion of non-maritime uses on the waterfront, while still prohibiting condos and other residential development. Alliance members were very disappointed when the council adopted a more restrictive zoning plan. Many are still angry at the unwillingness of the city's politicians to respect the product of an exhaustive stakeholder process.

A revised zoning plan adopted in 1993 put in place two new zones for the waterfront. The Waterfront Special Use zone stretches from the Maine State Pier on the east to the International Marine Terminal on the west. Here, first floor use is limited to maritime businesses. Above the first floor, 50 percent of the space can be non-maritime use. The more restrictive waterfront zone flanks the special use zone on both sides and permits only marine uses.

On the east, the waterfront zone goes from the Maine State Pier, through the BIW property now owned by the city, to the Portland Yacht Service marina and extends inland to Fore Street. Most the land in the waterfront zone not controlled by the city is owned by two developers, Bill Farley and Mike Marino. Because of the restrictive zoning, any mixed-use development of their property—or of the property the city acquired from BIW—would require changed zoning. On the west, the waterfront zone stretches from the International Marine Terminal to Merrill's Marine Terminal. Guilford Transportation is the primary owner of the long empty stretch between the two terminals. Many believe that Guilford is land-banking this extensive parcel, the largest undeveloped site on the Portland waterfront, because it is limited to marine uses under the 1993 zoning.

The city and state are beginning to recognize that a pier or wharf is not much different from an industrial park that needs public support. The city, using $1 million in seed money from the sale of the former BIW dry dock, recently set up a

Working Waterfront Loan Fund, administered by Coastal Enterprises Inc. Additional money will be generated through a tax increment financing (TIF) scheme on any waterfront project over $400,000. Targeting private pier owners, this revolving fund will provide low cost financing for dredging, pier maintenance, repair and environmental upgrades. Whether the loans will make financial sense to private pier owners remains to be seen. In addition, the Maine Department of Transportation is studying ways the public might share in the cost of dredging.

THE BIW LAND

Since recent waterfront policy has been shaped by the delicate balancing of competing forces, many see the former BIW land as an opportunity to develop a long-term vision for Portland waterfront that will be embraced by its citizens.

In January 2001, the city held a day-long meeting to develop alternate visions of the waterfront. Over 170 members of the public attended, from all walks of life. Public involvement and exchange continued through the year at committee meetings, council hearings and on a well-utilized website. Casco Bay islanders in particular participated actively in the process, which directly impacted their ferry terminal and parking.

Portland's mayor appointed two committees. A seven-member Facilities Committee was given the narrow charge of developing a plan for a project known as "Ocean Gateway," which called for reconstruction of the Maine State Pier and the BIW site ("Pier 2"), using $16.2 million in state bond money and $1 million for consultant studies. The Facilities Committee assumed, based on previous planning studies, that cruise ships and the international ferry should be consolidated at the east end of Commercial Street near the Casco Bay Ferry Terminal. With retail shops, offices and restaurants nearby on the land side of Commercial Street, this area invites pedestrians.

The Master Planning Committee had the broader charge of developing an overall plan for the former BIW parcel and its surrounding area. With over 30 members, it was unwieldy but included constituencies not represented on the Facilities Committee. The Master Planning Committee wrestled with the big problems: how to integrate development of the former Grand Trunk rail yards on the southwest flank of Munjoy Hill with adjacent residential and commercial areas, and how to mitigate negative impacts from ferry and passenger facilities and new development. Many on the committee believe that new development in the former Grand Trunk yards would have a greater impact than the Ocean Gateway facilities. The committee also focused on the needs of islanders, especially parking. They had only $50,000 from the city to pay for studies, and no money in hand to shape future development.

Yet, in November, when both committees reported to the City Council, they had arrived at remarkably similar proposals for the eastern end of Commercial Street. Both envisioned quality architecture of compatible scale and size to the rest of the city, along with public space, public access and marine use of the waterfront. The Maine State Pier and Pier 2 would service Casco Bay Ferry Lines, the SCOTIA PRINCE, cruise ships and high-speed ferries. Parking and lanes for cars boarding the SCOTIA PRINCE would be next to the ferry terminal. Plans included enlarging the Casco Bay Ferry Terminal, Portland's vital link to the islands. Commercial Street would extend farther east.

North of Commercial Street, the old railroad yards would be divided into a network of streets with the same scale and size as those in the adjacent Old Port. Three-and four-story brick buildings lining sidewalks would house retail, residential, and possibly a hotel and convention center. In each block, buildings wrap around interior parking garages.

In November 2001, the City Council referred both reports to the City Development Commission. The council will have to make the final decision on the scope and direction of this massive project.

City officials want to deal with congestion at the International Ferry Terminal by moving passenger facilities to the BIW site. New security measures deemed necessary after the Sept. 11 destruction of the World Trade Center Towers gave added weight to separating international passenger and cargo, as well as added expense. Officials worry that the $16.2 million earmarked for transportation issues will lose value as time wears on, and they feel pressure to get the job moving.

Many, however, see new city streets and buildings as an essential part of the area's development. They believe that this infrastructure will only be possible through several phases in a creative mix of public and private financing. In the history of Portland's waterfront development, inventive partnerships of public and private money have been key to the economic vitality of the waterfront.

The estimates for such development begin at $50 million and rise steeply. With no money in city coffers for this broader development and no clear plan, many are concerned that the BIW site will become acres of surface parking—a waste of prime waterfront property. Some hold that a convention center and hotel complex should be located elsewhere on the Portland peninsula, away from deepwater frontage. Others want any housing plans to include low and middle income units. Neighbors on Munjoy Hill worry about noise and congestion. Any non-marine uses will require a zoning change, which will undoubtedly bring strong debate.

The City Council will have to decide whether to go ahead with the Ocean

Portland doesn't have the luxury of much deep-water shoreline

Gateway facilities using the existing $16.2 million funding, or to first develop a comprehensive plan addressing the broader contentious issues.

Ben Snow, Manager, Marine Operations and Administration for Portland, pulls out books with glossy photos featuring other cities' "revitalized" waterfronts with office towers, broad open spaces and pedestrian walkways.

"It's great urban architecture right up to the waterfront," he says, "but it's all for pedestrians, and views for people on the land side."

These projects may represent "highest and best use" value in the short run, but do little to support a working waterfront in the long run, says Snow, "because they don't support the infrastructure such as wharves or tugs, things that a working port requires."

Other cities have moved marine industry out of the way to other parts of the harbor, but Portland doesn't have the luxury of much deepwater shoreline. Instead, through planning and neglect, foresight and luck, Portland is unmatched in having a real working waterfront in the heart of the city. And citizens seem to want to keep it like that.

Joan Amory, *who writes frequently for Island Institute publications, lives near the Portland waterfront.*

"It Hasteth Away"

A marriage survives island gossip,

but not war.

Sabrina Seely Brown in her early twenties.

RANDOLPH PURINTON

War correspondence ought to receive honors in the history of literature. Letters written between soldiers and their loved ones evoke expressions of drama and passion that should share literary acclaim alongside the works of playwrights and poets. If the greatest literature is remarkable because critics say that it expresses the truth of human experience, then war correspondence deserves the same consideration.

Often an exchange of letters concludes when a soldier returns home, but there's no guarantee a soldier will return and sometimes it simply ends. Then we know that behind the correspondence there was great conflict, suffering and loss. It may be the survivor who suffers most, because he or she retains the memory of departure, absence, death and loss.

Battlefield photograph courtesy of the Library of Congress.

Bull Run was the first major battle between Union and Confederate armies in northern Virginia. It was a test of the Union Army's leadership and training. The day ended with the rout of Union forces. Wesley Brown, a member of the Bangor Light Infantry in Maine's Second Division, survived the First Battle of Bull Run and wrote these lines on July 27, 1861, to his wife, Sabrina, on Islesboro:

...I would have wagered my life that we should conquer but it was not to be. For fear of your letters being seen by someone else in case I was shot I burnt every one of them and since that time have felt lonesome on that account so darling you must write a lot and send them to make up for those won't you.

Despite the loss of several of Sabrina's letters to her husband, the Civil War correspondence between Wesley and Sabrina Brown of Islesboro remains a comprehensive record of thoughts and feelings that passed between a young Maine soldier and his island wife. Sabrina's maiden name was Seely. John Seely, Sabrina's father, came from off-island and in 1834 married Phebe Veazie, whose family presence on Islesboro went back to 1785. Sabrina had four siblings. Much less is known of Wesley Brown's history, except that he probably grew up in Bangor. There was a Brown family on Islesboro during the 19th century, but Wesley may or may not have been related to them.

Sabrina was a daughter of the island. In a pre-Civil War letter that she wrote to Wesley, she shared her familiarity with the lives of island residents:

North Islesboro, April 24, 1860...Capt. Benjamin Warren was buried today. Mrs. Emiline Hatch is a raving maniac. She threw a cup of gruel in Rev. Burbank's face and came near putting his eye out—tore his hair off him etc. They have put her in a straight jacket. Edgar Bunker I understand broke his leg driving a pair of ugly steers, poor fellow. Mary Ann Dodge has got a beau. She never was going to get married, perhaps she won't, there is many a slip between cup and lip...

There is much less island news in the Civil War correspondence. But months after Wesley left the state as a soldier in Maine's Second Division, the letters reveal that island gossip threatened the integrity of Wesley and Sabrina's brief marriage.

Fortunately, only two months passed between the time that Wesley left Maine to the day he wrote the letter about the retreat from Bull Run. The bulk of the collection—housed in the Islesboro Historical Society—begins soon after Wesley enlisted in April 1861, and ends in September 1862. The letters were among materials donated to the Historical Society in 1994 by descendants of Sabrina's. For at least a century the 35 or so letters were among other papers stored in Gablewood, the house that Sabrina and her second husband, Fields C. Pendleton, built on Islesboro. Bunny Logan, president of the society, said that these materials came in "seven boxes and a bag" and that as of last winter, she hadn't yet processed the complete donation.

Wesley and Sabrina initiated a correspondence at least a year before they married. Sometime around March 1860, a vow or pledge passed between them. Two weeks after a visit to the island, Wesley was seeking work in the Lewiston-Auburn area and feeling discouraged because he was unemployed. He believed that a husband ought to provide for his wife, and he extended to Sabrina the option of releasing herself from her vow if she felt uncertain about Wesley's ability to support her. On April 16, 1860, he wrote to Sabrina:

Dear Friend, I feel that is my duty (being such friends) to inform you of my prospects, so that you may do nothing that you may afterwards regret. I am now without work as I have been since my arrival here, but I hope soon to get some of some kind ... My object in writing the above is that I sometimes fear that you may regret what has passed between us and wish it annulled, if so 'tis in your power to do it. But, Dear Girl, I had rather hear of the death of my best friend that you should do so. Mine, Sabrina, is a nature that loves but once, and that love is centered in you ...if my prospects were better I should wish that we might be married this fall (don't blush) if you would consent to it, but as I am situated it would be folly for me to ask it of you as I have no home to take

you ... Say, did you ever think of having Wesley for a husband! Do you think that he could earn enough to support Brina as she should be so that she would not be obliged to work ...I'm sure he would do it if Brina would consent to it....

Wesley's advice to Sabrina not to blush suggests that talk of marriage had not been discussed prior to this letter, although something might have passed between them two weeks before on the island—an agreement that could be annulled—and that would lead one to assume that marriage would follow. Sabrina responded the following week:

...I fancy that you misjudge me if you think for one moment that I wish annulled what has passed between us. No, Wesley, I don't wish it and it would take more than anything so transient as money to cause me to wish otherwise. I have took pleasure in your society, been happy thinking you my friend.... I am myself such not only in Prosperity but also when the cold winds of adversity blow.... You won't be discouraged that life may look gloomy now and then. There is sunshine in store for you yet:

Be cheerful and happy
Have joy while you can
Life cannot last always
It hasteth away—

Wesley and Sabrina married Thursday, March 28, 1861, on Islesboro. On the same day Wesley's cousin Henry Wheeler wrote to him from Bangor, wanting to know "all the particulars." Fifteen days later, Fort Sumter was bombarded. On April 15, President Lincoln called for troops from states loyal to the Union. Cousin Henry again wrote to Wesley on April 21:

Sabrina was buried in Isleboro next to her second husband, Fields Pendleton.

Sabrina later in life, at Gablewood, her house on Islesboro.

…What is your state of mind at this time? I hope that you feel willing to serve your country even to the death …. Two days ago a recruiting office opened here and they have raised a company of seventy-five men … I think I will go into the Light Infantry if I can … I suppose that Brina will not let you go, will she?

Both Henry and Wesley enlisted in the Bangor Light Infantry of the Second Division, as did Wesley's brother, George. It was exactly a year after Sabrina's positive response to Wesley's proposal that the husband and wife parted. They had lived together as a married couple on Islesboro only 27 days.

Wesley became one among tens of thousands of soldiers who fought in skirmishes and battles in the region between Washington, D.C., and Richmond, Virginia. During the first battle of Bull Run, Wesley saved the life of a sun-struck and delirious Castine man who would surely have been taken prisoner or killed outright had Wesley not shouldered and cared for him during the long retreat back toward the capital. Wesley wrote about the ordeal and regretted not being able to snatch a few rebel guns for his own use or as souvenirs because he was occupied in a humanitarian effort. The man's mother later wrote a touching letter to Wesley, thanking him for saving her son's life:

Aug. 18, 1861… May God's richest blessings rest on you and yours forever and should you ever need a friend may you find such a one that you proved yourself, the noblest deed a man can do, casting aside self in an hour of peril, to aid your suffering friend when men were fleeing to save the little life that was left after that horrid day … accept a mother's blessing who will pray for you ever. Your friend, Mrs. Sewall Perkins.

It was around this time that Wesley was thinking about his own vulnerability. After all, it is only luck that spares soldiers from injury and death. Wesley had seen enough of battle to know that he could be seriously injured and could have to depend on another to be led off the field or to be taken care of for the rest of his life. It was during a moment of reflection about these concerns that he wrote Sabrina these lines:

I cannot keep the foolish thought from my head that if I should return to you maimed, disfigured, perhaps lame for life that you would not love me as well as you do now; that together with my rough associations of mind and matter will I fear unfit for you as a companion. My own precious one if I have done wrong in writing the above please to excuse me and when I get home Brina shall pull my ears real hard to pay for it… PS: I have looked over the above and see how foolish I am… Don't pay any attention to it and believe me as ever your loving husband, Wesley.

Five months after Wesley left Islesboro, Sabrina became deeply troubled by a piece of island gossip. Wesley must have sensed her distress because of the tone of her most recent letter. In his next letter Wesley questioned his wife concerning the source of her grief and tried to reassure her that whatever lie was being spread around it couldn't be any worse than the usual brand of island gossip.

…But darling you must not be paying attention to such idle gossip as I know abounds in Islesboro, at all times … the ones that talk like that are no more worthy of notice of Brina than Jeff Davis is to sit in Lincoln's seat and them same persons are worse traitors than Jeff is for they, under the guise of friendship, assail in the tenderest part of a person's character while Davis comes out in open warfare…

Wesley was not aware of the gravity of the most recent gossip; that Wesley left Sabrina to join the Union Army because he was dissatisfied with his wife and married life. Sabrina had to confront her husband:

…allow me to ask a question…do you think that you could be happy with me, were you always happy after our marriage and did you never sigh for single blessedness, and wish that thyself and Brina had remained twain forever … did you ever say to any person walking this earth that I was not suited for married life and unhappiness with me was the chief cause of your enlistment… Wesley, I implore you in the name of all that's good to tell me if ever such escaped your lips. Wesley, if ever there was anything that made me unhappy, yea wretched, it was that…

Wesley responded:

As I hope for salvation, I never said aught like that to any being, never thought like that anything of the kind and had I done so, never should have said it to anyone… May God direct the first ball that is fired straight to my heart and may my soul forever remain in punishment if I have ever said anything of the kind… The happiest month of my life was from the 28th of March to the 24th of April, 1861… It was not because I did not enjoy the married life that I enlisted; it was because I loved my country and was willing to sacrifice the newfound joy of life and everything for her, my country's honor. It was the hardest thing I ever done…

There's no reason to think that Wesley enlisted for anything other than patriotic reasons. All we need to do is read Henry's letter to his cousin to sense the depth of loyalty Maine men attached to the Union—a loyalty that demanded, if necessary, the sacrifice of one's life. There being no children might have made the decision to enlist a little easier. Wesley's decision was not made without balancing the joys of married life with the risks inherent in defending his country's honor. After all, he did say that deciding to join was "the hardest thing [he had] ever done."

Wesley's love for Sabrina sustained his life at least once. After the retreat from Bull Run he wrote, "We marched between 50 and 60 miles without food or rest, and the only wonder to me is how we stood it, but the thoughts of friends sustained many, I know it did for me for if there had been no Brina to have mourned my loss I should have given up." Wesley's dependency upon Brina's love during that crisis speaks of an enduring union.

It is true that Wesley was impressed with the larger world, away from the island. When he was passing through New York Harbor he saw the GREAT EASTERN, the largest ship of its time. A failure as a luxury passenger vessel, the GREAT EASTERN was later refitted to lay the first transatlantic cable. In Chesapeake Bay, he saw the MONITOR, the Union ironclad warship of revolutionary design. He was a soldier among thousands who boarded a hundred steamships during a troop movement down the Potomac. They passed Mt. Vernon on their way. He stood at attention as Lincoln inspected the troops in his company during a Grand Review. He stayed by his brother's side for four days while awaiting medical attention because George had shattered his ankle during combat and couldn't walk. Clara Barton, the legendary caregiver and founder of the American Red Cross, made her debut on the battlefields in the same region where Wesley was wounded. He was at the center of history for a while, but as we all know, the more battles a soldier survives the closer he gets to that battle when his luck runs out. In August 1862, Wesley was running low on luck.

Wesley had hoped to march into Richmond, Virginia, as a soldier in a victorious Union army. Instead, he spent time in Richmond as a prisoner but was returned to his company during a regular exchange of Union and Confederate soldiers. He lost weight during his imprisonment, but was otherwise healthy so he was not privileged to return home for rest as he had hoped. Ironically, the last letter he wrote before he was captured included the line, "I was sorry to hear that such an absurd story as that I was a prisoner was afloat in Islesboro; so far from the truth as you can think…" Two days later, while that letter was still in transit, Wesley was captured. He spent a month in prison and was exchanged on August 6. Immediately after he was released he wrote a short letter to Sabrina:

…I got back to my regiment last night at ten o'clock. We have had rather a hard time of it … but we will call that one of the vicissitudes of a soldier's life and so let it pass… I did

some expect to have the pleasure of meeting you this fall but now I do not…

In his last letter to Sabrina, Wesley says that he had received no letters from her after he was released. One hopes Wesley eventually received Sabrina's last two letters, because they are her best and most urgent. Because these two letters survive in the Islesboro collection, Wesley must have received and read them before he died. After hearing he had been released, Sabrina wrote:

… For a time I really looked for you at home, and used to watch the Packet and stage as much as though I had received a direct dispatch from you … but never mind, Brina will wait but O I want to see you so much and it seems kind of hard, but after all this there is a time coming is there not dearest and I know of someone who can look beyond the gloomy present to a bright and joyous future which I trust may in a measure compensate for the gloomy past…

But that bright and joyous future never came. Wesley's luck ran out at the battle of Groveton on August 30, 1862, one of many pre-Gettysburg battles that took place in the region between Washington and Richmond. Groveton was part of the second Battle of Bull Run. Fatally wounded, Wesley was taken to the Baptist Church Hospital in Alexandria, Virginia. It was there that he wrote this last, short letter to his island wife:

Dear Brina, I have at last met with a soldier's fate but fortunately I guess I will recover and then peace and quiet with my Brina at home. I am very weak but my wound is going well. I have not as yet heard from you since I went to Richmond—I shall not be able to know for a month yet, write to me as soon as you get this. I wrote to you about sending one a day.

Brina's last letter is from Bangor, September 13:

…I wish it was in my power to care of you. I should be so happy if I could… Though it would pain me to see you suffering yet I should know to what extent you suffered and would be so tender of you. O I know that none could nurse you more tenderly and none could anticipate your every wish more readily than I … but I will patiently wait putting my trust in him who doeth all for the best though he works in a mysterious way… There has been suffering sufficient already to have saved a nation… It does distress me to think of it and for you suffering long without any assistance seems almost intolerable. It will disgrace the pages of American history. I have read of our soldiers being left to suffer that length of time before but Heaven knows that it never came quite so near before….

I hope dearest you will excuse this letter and forgive if I have said ought too much—dearest how can I help it when you have endured so much suffering with thousands of others and all; I was going to say "for nothing." The majority of people here are losing all confidence in Government… Wesley write me just as often as you can if no more than a line so I can know how you get along and come home as soon as you are able to be moved so I can take care of you myself on my own bed. Bless your life how I love you dear precious sufferer. Keep up good courage my darling and O don't _____ and leave Brina all alone…

Wesley died ten days later from the wound he received at Groveton. Though the bodies of many Union soldiers were returned home and buried by their families, Wesley's body was not. Sometimes financial considerations decided whether or not a body would be shipped north. Wesley's body was removed from the Baptist Church Hospital and was buried in a soldiers' cemetery in Alexandria, Virginia. Sabrina's letters to Wesley were sent to Sabrina by George Brown, Wesley's brother, who visited the hospital during his return south to his regiment after a period of convalescence with his wife in Castine.

In 1863, a year after Wesley's death, Sabrina gave her blessing upon the marriage of her younger sister, Lucinda, 19, and Islesboro resident Fields C. Pendleton, 31, a ship master and owner. Lucinda died two years later in 1865. In 1866 Sabrina, then 26, married Fields—her sister's husband—and they had eight children over a period of sixteen years. One of Sabrina's daughters, Alice L. Pendleton, was the first librarian of the Islesboro Free Library and her name is chiseled in stone above the front door of that building. Sabrina and Fields are buried next to each other in the Pendleton family cemetery on Islesboro.

People say that a dying person sees his life pass before him. Perhaps Wesley experienced the same. If so, a particular letter might have drifted into his fading field of vision, the one at the end of which Sabrina wrote a short poem:

In pleasures, dreams or sorrows hour
In crowded hall or lonely bower
The object of my life shall be
Forever to remember thee.

Randolph Purinton is chaplain of the Williston Northampton School. Photos of Sabrina courtesy of the Islesboro Historical Society.

The Spirit of the Grass

Continued from page 17

those stranded by shipwreck. That year, the Humane Establishment was founded, and would spend the next 157 years saving the lives and cargoes of 222 shipwrecks on Sable.

The lifesavers and their families were expected to feed themselves on Sable, and grew vegetables and raised cattle, pigs and poultry. They grew their own hay, and gathered driftwood and ship timbers for fuel. Three lifesaving stations were spread across the island, and a boarding school was established at Station 2 for the island children to attend, if and when a tutor was available.

The advent of radar, fathometers and other modern technology made shipwrecks on Sable obsolete by the 1950s, and in 1958 the Humane Establishment closed its doors. When the last families to live on the island left in the late 1960s, the human presence on the island was focused purely on conservation efforts.

Weather observations on Sable Island have been continuous since 1891, making it the longest continuous data collection in Canada. In 1971, Environment Canada took over the operation of the Atmospheric Research and Weather Station on Sable, which records weather patterns and upper air atmospheric conditions through research and weather balloons.

By the mid-1990s, the cost of running the station and maintaining the human resources it required became prohibitive, and the federal agency began to search for organizations to help contribute to the financial needs of the station. In March 2000, the Sable Island Preservation Trust assumed responsibility for managing the island and the weather station. The nonprofit trust is funded by two major oil corporations, Pan Canadian Resources and Exxon-Mobil, as well as the province of Nova Scotia.

Funding for the island from offshore oil corporations has raised the hackles of environmental groups, who fought against the "Sable Island Industrial Park": two monstrous rigs drilling for natural gas and oil just a few miles from Sable Island. Installed four years ago by the same companies that provide financial support to the Trust, the rigs were the first in the area. While the rigs provide employment for a province short on jobs, they also raise fears about the expansion of oil explo-

Sable Island weather station.

ration and drilling around the environmentally sensitive island, and within the Scotian Shelf, an oceanic valley with great potential for oil reserves.

"We are afraid of the cumulative impact this may have on the island and on the surrounding ocean waters," says Mark Butler of Ecology Action, a nonprofit environmental protection organization. "It opens the door to more oil operations in the area, and sends the message that Nova Scotia is open for this kind of business."

From the south beach, it's impossible not to notice the rigs. They sit heavy on the horizon, a black arm of smoke stretching from the stack of one rig clear across the island, reaching for the horizon and refusing to dissipate.

Even with the support of large corporations, operating costs for the island are still dangerously high. The Trust barely made it through the last fiscal year, and is currently re-negotiating the contract it has with Environment Canada, the Coast Guard and the Department of the Environment. In a worst-case scenario, the weather station would be closed down, and the human presence on the island would no longer be necessary or viable. All parties agree that losing the weather station and the human presence it requires would be a disaster for Sable.

But for Zoe Lucas and the island itself, life goes on. The dune restoration project that first brought her to Sable in 1971 evolved into a lifetime of living on an extraordinary island, among a unique population of horses—a study that at one time required her to collect and haul over 6,000 pounds of horse manure.

These days, she is focused on a long-term genetic study of the horses, collecting the skulls, teeth and bones for measurements and analysis. That is what has brought us to a marshy area near one of the island's freshwater ponds. Walking towards the pond, we suddenly come upon a extraordinarily verdant patch of grass

and roses. In the middle of it is a horse, almost completely decomposed.

Almost.

Next thing I know, I am on my knees, digging with my hands through thousands of empty black maggot cases, and the remains of the horse's stomach—including what was in it when he died. Among the bones and flies there are blond curls of his mane, still long and beautiful and tangled.

Zoe and I work together, pulling out each and every bone with great care. When we are finished there is barely anything left. Within a few weeks it will be entirely grown over, leaving no evidence of the horse that lived and died here. So this is what happens when a horse dies, I thought.

But what happens to the spirit of the horse? I look over my shoulder to see a young foal with a mouthful of green blades, and I know that I believe Zoe when she tells me: it becomes the spirit of the grass.

As one of an increasingly small number of such places, Sable Island is still a place where the natural rhythms of life and death remain relatively unchallenged by human intervention. Zoe Lucas has spent a lifetime in quiet observation, and contemplation, of these rhythms. The horses here, and the seals; the birds and the sharks; the endless stretches of grass and surf; this is what Henry Beston meant when he wrote about "other nations."

For Zoe, living on Sable Island has meant living as a nation of one. And to live respectfully with nations she cannot make assumptions about, Zoe has instead lived among them as though she herself were merely a ghost who prowled the dunes.

Katie Vaux is a freelance writer based in Nova Scotia. Photos by *Zoe Lucas*.

"Mighty Salty"

The Long and Curious Career of the
CORA F. CRESSY

STEVE CARTWRIGHT

Launching day, 1902

This is the story of a Maine-built, gaff-rigged schooner with sweeping sheer, high bow, deep hull and a long working life carrying cargoes of coal, steel, ice and floating nightclub patrons. Even today the vessel that earned the name "Queen of the Atlantic" serves a useful purpose: a breakwater for a Muscongus Bay wharf and lobster pound.

One hundred years ago, the CORA F. CRESSY slipped down the ways at the Percy & Small Shipyard in Bath. Today the CRESSY lies at Keene's Neck, where her spiked hull timbers are giving way, exposing seaweed-covered lower decks and beams, rusting iron chainplates and tamarack knees. Only the bow still has a ship's shape and still hints at the immensity of the old CRESSY. She might yet inspire awe, but her graceful, seaworthy curves are long gone.

The CRESSY was nothing if not a survivor. She weathered a gale in which her larger sister schooner, the WYOMING, sank. She survived being abandoned and looted off Searsport. She survived plans to burn her at sea. *The Portland Evening Express* reported in February 1938 that "instead of rotting on some backwater creek, the once proud sailing vessel will be towed out to sea and a torch applied." It didn't happen. Instead, the late Bernard "Bunny" Zahn bought the CRESSY for $200 and had her towed from Boston to his lobster pound—her last trip ever.

If anyone ever considered turning the CRESSY into a museum, there is no reliable record of it. Zahn once said he would give the schooner away, but by then it was too late. Instead, pieces of the CRESSY have been preserved in museums and private homes. There are records, too, such as the journal of the late Russell Seaver, who as a Harvard student, signed on for CRESSY's final passage under sail:

"Friday, Aug. 31, 1928: Reported aboard CORA CRESSY (in Bangor) at 8 a.m. to find I had secured able-bodied seaman's job. Quite delirious but a little confused as to what to tell the chief engineer of the HALL who was expecting me to finish my day's work there."

Before taking leave in Boston on Sept. 10, during his last night aboard, Seaver hacked off a chunk of overhead beam where some earlier sailor had carefully etched the CRESSY under full sail. In his 70s, Seaver gave the carving to the Maine Maritime Museum, which already displayed CRESSY's billethead at its front door. The museum also has a carved name board and stateroom paneling removed from the CRESSY, which seems highly appropriate for a museum that also incorporates the preserved Percy & Small shipyard. That's where the CORA CRESSY was launched April 12, 1902.

At close to 300 feet from stem to stern, she was one of the larger and more profitable of the 45 schooners launched by the P & S yard. The CRESSY had a 4,000-ton coal carrying capacity, and was said to have the highest bow on the coast—that's how mariners recognized her from afar. She was long, deep and wide; her Oregon pine

The massive mast of the CRESSEY. Photo from the collection of Douglas K. and Linda T. Lee.

A CRESSY Chronology

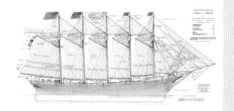

April 12, 1902
CORA F. CRESSY is launched into the Kennebec River by her builder, the Percy & Small shipyard of Bath.

March 27, 1903
The five-masted CRESSY beats the six-masted ADDIE M. LAWRENCE on a passage from Norfolk to Portland with cargoes of coal—even though the CRESSY departed several days after her P&S-built rival.

March 27, 1904
The CRESSY and a steamboat arrive in Philadelphia, after colliding the previous Saturday off Five Fathom Bank lightship during fog.

masts were 118 feet tall, 30 inches in diameter, and topmasts added another 54 feet, for a towering total of 173 feet from keel to tip of topmast.

The Bath Daily Times of April 12, 1902, reported, "The handsome new five-masted schooner CORA F. CRESSY was successfully launched at 2:30 p.m. from the yard of Percy & Small...the craft made a pretty plunge into the Kennebec amid the salutes of the whistles on shore and from the tug KNICKERBOCKER." Cora Cressy, wife of co-owner and coal dealer Myron Cressy of Boston, christened the vessel. The Times said the schooner's frames were white oak, her middle deck yellow pine and her upper deck, white pine. The ship's planking was five inches thick, with two steel "hog straps" running fore and aft, a foot wide and nearly inch thick. CRESSY could carry 8,000 square yards of sail. The officers' cabin was

finished in oak, black walnut and curly cypress.

An innovation, the paper said, was a yawl boat powered by a Palmer gas engine, for the captain's use while in port.

The forecastle was part of a 27- by 30-foot forward deck house that included the hoisting room and carpenter's shop. Despite the vastness of the CRESSY, she was built to sail with a crew of 12 men.

CRESSY was reportedly quirky sailing to windward with an empty hold, so 300 tons of sand ballast were added. "She was so high-sided she nearly sailed on her side, so they put ballast in her within a year of when she was built," said Ralph L. Snow, former head of the Maine Maritime Museum in Bath. She sailed like a dream when loaded, her skippers reported.

In her first couple of decades, carrying 4,000 tons of coal to coastal ports, CRESSY brought a very substantial return to her

CRESSY as a Boston nightclub in the 1930s, when she was known as Levaggi's Showboat. Photo from the collection of Douglas K. and Linda T. Lee.

owners, which included Percy & Small for her first 18 years. "I guess one would say of the CRESSY, she was a lucky vessel," said Snow. "As far as I know, she was the largest intact wooden sailing hull in the world...but you can't say that now."

"Sept. 1, 1928: The tug brought a four-mast schooner from up the river. Then, after undocking the HALL and starting her down the river ahead of us, returned to lash the two schooners (the other was the LUCIA P. DOW) side by side to make a neat towing package.

The passage down the Penobscot went smoothly, and a mile beyond Fort Point we all cast off our various lines and were on our own. There was a stiff breeze blowing in from

---

September 7, 1904

The Bath Daily Times quotes a Newport News Press report that CRESSY Captain Haskell has bought two hogs, 42 chickens, two dogs, 14 pigeons, 10 white mice and other livestock, and brought all on board.

April 5, 1904

The CRESSY, bound for Newport News, is towed into Fortress Monroe with a lost jib boom and damaged stern.

May 12, 1904

Seven former CRESSY crew members file suit for $5,000, claiming they were shanghaied and shackled to the ship.

March 11, 1924

The five-masted CRESSY and six-masted WYOMING are both anchored on Nantucket shoals as a gale-driven blizzard intensifies. CRESSY weighs anchor and sails off to ride out the storm in deeper water. WYOMING sinks with all hands.

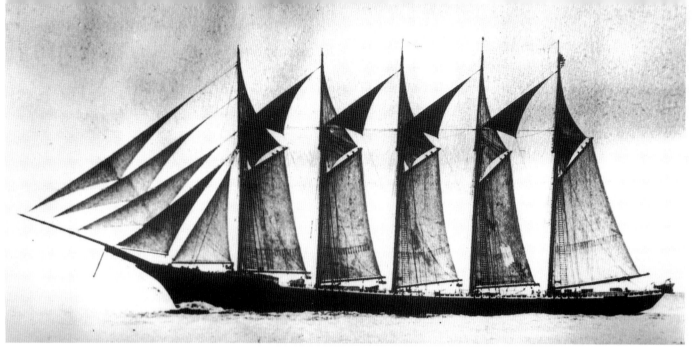

CRESSY under full sail, topmasts still in place, in the 1920s. She enjoyed a reputation for stout seaworthiness. Photo courtesy of the Maine Maritime Museum.

Penobscot Bay and open sea beyond. We immediately commenced hoisting our five large lower sails...[the LUCIA DOW's captain] was a great rival of our Captain Brown in the point of sailing. But we were superior for the first day as we anchored three miles ahead of him after much tacking and maneuvering by both ships."

Unlike her contemporaries—schooners that sank or were scrapped—the CRESSY lasted on and on, making her the sole surviving five-master of her kind in the world. "She had a lot of problems over the course of her lifetime," said Maine Maritime Museum librarian Nathan Lipfert. "Yet she survived all of that. Not exactly looking like a rose, but she survived."

Lipfert recalled a couple of gales that nearly ended the CRESSY's career. On March 11, 1924, the CRESSY, along with the six-master WYOMING, largest schooner built by Percy & Small, anchored on Pollock Rip shoals as a Northeaster pounded the two vessels, a blizzard swirling around them. The wind and seas rose, and Capt. Charles Publicover of the CRESSY decided to weigh anchor, set sail and head for deep water. The CRESSY weathered the big storm, but the WYOMING was lost with all hands.

Capt. Doug Lee, a CRESSY authority and master of the Rockland windjammer HERITAGE, believes WYOMING was sunk when an unmanned barge broke loose from its tow-line and rammed the big schooner. The barge was never recovered. Meanwhile, the CRESSY's reputation for stout seaworthiness spread.

"She survived the ravages of the sea because of her design," said Lee. Prominently displayed in Lee's home is a gold-leaf, carved quarter board taken from the CRESSY. Lee explained that the CRESSY's long life, even in irreversible decay, provided him and others with a magnificent opportunity for hands-on study of how a great schooner was constructed. The original builders probably lofted the CRESSY's design from a half model, without any naval architectural drawings.

"Sept. 2, 1928: The wheezing donkey engine is just able to bring the anchor home, but Jim and I must clamber down to the chain locker to coil down the mud-caked links as they come clanking inexorably down upon us. Four men have been killed here when chains parted or windlasses failed, allowing the chain to go roaring back up the hawsepipe. Our single lantern shows us the ancient ladder that takes us down for about 40 feet. The last 20 feet, we shinny down the chain itself until we end in the very bowels of the hull where we feed the clanking chain into a grave-shaped bin as neatly as we can.

"We spent the day tacking back and forth across Penobscot Bay into a brisk head-wind. We must have covered 50 miles north and south to make a good 10 miles toward Monhegan Island."

Today, the CRESSY is going the way of the HESPER and LUTHER LITTLE, four-masted schooners that for decades were a fixture in the mud of Wiscasset. Like the CRESSY they were victims, in their old age, of complete neglect. Lee said that Zahn even tried to buy the LITTLE when she was still afloat, before he found the larger CRESSY.

Where 20 years ago you could walk her deck, carefully avoiding rotten spots, today there is no deck. One side of the hull has caved in, leaving a yawning breach, exposing lower deck beams. Everywhere there are soggy, rotting, seaweed-covered timbers. With each passing year those rugged old beams and planks look less and less like a schooner, let alone "Queen of the Atlantic," as the *Boston Herald* called her after she weathered the storm off Pollock Rip shoals.

Not long ago, the town fire department answered a call about fire on the CRESSY, which had spread from a burning lobster boat. Damage to the old schooner was negligible.

"Sept. 3, 1928: Overcast skies and a favorable wind but a broken down donkey engine, without which we could move neither sails nor

---

April, 1925

Hard times force the sale of **CRESSY** at a U.S. Marshal's auction in Portland.

December, 1925

The **CRESSY** is blown off course in continuing heavy weather after heading south from Boston, and for weeks there is no word of her. Finally, the battered **CRESSY** arrives in Florida, although the coal port of Norfolk was her destination.

1926

CRESSY's skipper, Captain Frank Perkins of Blue Hill, sailing short-handed, goes forward to help hoist a sail and falls to his death through an open hatch.

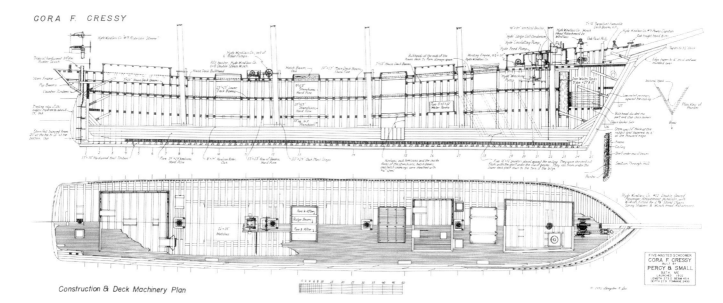

CORA F. CRESSY

Construction & Deck Machinery Plan

FIVE-MASTED SCHOONER
CORA F. CRESSY
BUILT BY
PERCY & SMALL
BATH, ME.

anchor. *(The* LUCIA DOW *scudded past* CRESSY.) *We had one glorious tussle in a squall of rain getting the mainsail down. There is a thrill to flapping canvas and wildly swinging booms the size of telephone poles."*

The CRESSY survived, strangely, not just because of superior design and construction, but because of Prohibition and later, because Zahn, the lobster dealer, bought the now-shabby CRESSY in 1938, sold her masts and chain, and towed the tired schooner to his wharf and pound at Keene's Neck in Bremen. He surely made money on the deal; old-timers say selling the masts alone—for use as "camels" between dock and ship—more than covered the purchase cost.

Among the close calls for the CRESSY was in 1927. In February, the big schooner was damaged in a Jersey coast storm, then towed to Searsport, Maine, with a cargo of coal. After she was unloaded, she was anchored in the outer harbor and abandoned by captain and crew, the newspapers reported. She was left without lights—illegal under navigation laws—and without a watchman. Looters stripped her of hardware worth as much as $2,000.

On Oct. 13, 1927, CRESSY was driven onto a ledge "by the worst gale that has raged along this part of the coast within the memory of the oldest mariners," as a *Portland Press Herald* story put it. "The veteran craft, which was piled up in an unusually high tide, is listing to the star-

board tonight, but she shows no signs of breaking up."

Indeed not. A few days later, the cutter KICKAPOO from Rockland steamed to Searsport and hauled the derelict CRESSY off the ledge. By November, Capt. H.W. Frost of Portland arrived in Belfast to take charge of the refloated schooner, and have her refitted in that port or Rockland.

But long before the CORA CRESSY was warped into her final, shallow resting place, she underwent an expensive, exotic overhaul. In 1929, Boston entrepreneur Frederick Kaufman transformed the CRESSY into what many believe was a floating speakeasy during Prohibition. With tugs to nudge the schooner-turned-nightclub beyond the three-mile limit, legend has it that the liquor flowed and dancing girls did more than just dance, if male patrons were willing to pay for it. The booze and prostitution are undocumented, but not unlikely for a floating nightclub during Prohibition, enacted in 1920 and repealed 13 years later.

Named for manager John J. Levaggi of Lido-Venice and Terrace Gardens eateries, the CRESSY became LEVAGGI'S SHOWBOAT, a name you could still read on the transom before it rotted and collapsed some years ago.

"Sept. 5, 1928: Up at 5 this morning to take advantage of the long-awaited breeze from the north. After some trouble getting the anchor

properly home, we got under way with every stitch of sail set, which meant my first ascent to the topmasts to haul in and secure the topsails. The skipper had cannily waited until I had reached the masthead—at the base of the topmast—the higher one gets the harder it is to grasp anything firmly—your fingers seem to lack muscle and the clutch is hopelessness based upon panic."

The Boston Post headlined the CRESSY as "Boston's Own Ship of Pleasure," and the story puffed about "afternoon tea and bridge parties" and waiters in blue sailor suits. The grand opening, June 1, was to feature the Charles Hector orchestra.

In the supposedly luxurious conversion, CRESSY's topmasts were shortened—she never actually sailed again—and her main deck was almost entirely covered by a one-story frame building with French windows, its roof a 250-by 400-foot promenade deck. According to one newspaper story, the SHOWBOAT promised to be "an important feature of summertime gaiety in Boston."

At some point in her SHOWBOAT career, bare-breasted mermaids were painted on CRESSY's stairwell walls. Those buxom females were still visible in the 1960s. The story goes that fishermen working for Zahn painted a bra on each mermaid, so Zahn's wife, Nancy, wouldn't be offended.

▌ April 6, 1927

Newspapers report the **CRESSY**, at anchor for months at Searsport, is listing badly, half full of water, her rigging cut. The vessel has been ransacked, "evidently a victim of modern pirates," said the Portland Press Herald. The unlighted vessel is called a menace to navigation.

▌ October 13, 1927

The Press Herald reports the leaking **CRESSY** was beached on a ledge by a storm tide during "the worst gale that has raged along this part of the coast within the memory of the oldest mariners." The paper speculates this "may prove her last resting place."

▌ October 17, 1927

The Press Herald reports the **CRESSY** pulled off the ledge at Searsport by the cutter **KICKAPOO** from Rockland.

CRESSY docked at the Winnisimmet Shipyard in Chelsea, Mass.

"Sept. 6, 1928: A day of flat, oily calm. We painted and listened to the sobbing of innumerable blackfish."

After repeal, SHOWBOAT appeared doomed. *The Boston Traveler* of Feb. 25, 1938, reported "funeral services for a queen" were planned: "Soon the once proud sailing ship will start on her last voyage. Stripped of her white sails, rugged rigging and even the five tall masts, the schooner—now a deserted nightclub— will be towed by a tug out into the sea beyond Boston harbor and there set afire."

The real story was different. News of the CRESSY's impending inferno reached Bunny Zahn, a Brooklyn, N.Y., native who had decided to settle into his family's Maine home. As Zahn told it, one reason he could buy the CRESSY so cheaply is that she seemed to leak badly. A steam pump ran continuously. Zahn called Sam Percy, of Percy & Small, and Percy suggested he check to see if a seacock was open. Zahn hired a diver who found the valve open, water gushing in. He plugged it, and supposedly you could then bail the CRESSY with a teacup.

As soon as Zahn stopped the leak, he ran to the bank and sealed his $200 offer, then ordered the pump off his new boat. CRESSY and crew arrived in Muscongus Bay safe and dirty.

At Keene's Neck, Zahn extended a dock to a door cut in CRESSY's topsides, and he built an office on board. He at first packed and shipped lobsters from the schooner, but found this arrangement inconvenient. He left the schooner for an on-shore building.

Perhaps not all things attributed to the CRESSY are true. An article some years ago by John Cayford, in *Sea Classics* magazine, says the vessel was "still serviceable" in 1956, when CRESSY had been sitting in the mud for many years without maintenance. Cayford made an impassioned plea for salvaging CRESSY as a museum, even claiming a nonprofit organization had been formed with former Sen. Margaret Chase Smith serving on its board. No one today seems to recall any such group.

"Sept. 7, 1928: Made about five miles since Thursday noon, according to our patent log whose line drooped inertly over the poop-deck rail."

November 17, 1927

Capt. H.W. Frost of Portland takes command of the "derelict" **CRESSY** in Belfast.

September 1–10, 1928

Final voyage under sail for the **CORA F. CRESSY**, from Bangor to Boston. At the time she was reputed to be the largest working sailing vessel in the world.

June 1, 1929

Dedication of John J. Levaggi's Show Boat, the **CRESSY** converted from collier to restaurant, night club— and as legend holds, speakeasy.

If CRESSY saw duty as a speakeasy during Prohibition, serving booze on board, it wasn't the only illegal activity that took place under the schooner's nose.

As darkness fell on Nov. 13, 1982, a 77-foot Colombian freighter, the INDOMABLE, slipped into Zahn's cove with a cargo of more than 30 tons of marijuana, to be off-loaded to trucks alongside the old schooner. Police were tipped off, and the subsequent bust became a statewide story. Zahn denied all knowledge of the activity, although the trucks picking up the bales had to drive past his house to reach his dock.

A Maine State Trooper staking out the drug delivery saw Zahn's house lights flash, an apparent signal to the freighter. Lights flicked on and off "in a rapid manner," he said.

Doug Lee, who visited Zahn after he and his second wife, Dolly, moved—or fled—to Florida, said Zahn was too smart not to know about the drug shipment. "Nothing ever happened at Zahn's wharf that he didn't know about," Lee said. Zahn and his wife have since died.

Muscongus lobstermen scoff at the idea Zahn wasn't involved in the drug deal. "Of course he knew it, he was the one making the money," said Bremen Harbormaster Gilbert Collamore, a former selectman. Zahn knew how many lobsters he had in his pound; he would know if someone was unloading a boat at his wharf.

Stories of great schooners such as the CORA CRESSY are often told by marine historians, journalists and sometimes by former ships' officers. Much rarer are accounts such as Russell Seaver's first-person journal.

"Sept. 8, 1928: We have now drifted as far as Cape Ann, just north of Gloucester, and still no wind above a fitful breeze. These last two nights have been glorious, with a waning moon making stupendous ghosts of our sails—five of them in a solemn row, swinging eerily from side to side...last night I kept my bow lookout curled

up in the furled jibsail out at the tip of the 60-foot bowsprit. It was cozy and snug and quite detached from the rest of the vessel."

Sometimes a newspaper account revealed a darker side of life at sea. In 1904, two years after CRESSY's launching, the *Boston Post* reported that seven sailors were suing CRESSY's owners for $5,000, alleging they were shackled and held on board ship by the schooner's first captain, William Harding. He is said to have locked them in the lazarette for 24 hours—if true, a case of being shanghaied.

A lighter report that same year, published in the *Newport News Daily Press*, detailed how CRESSY's skipper, Capt. Ellis Haskell of Tenants Harbor, bought and brought on board 42 chickens and other livestock, while anchored on the James River. A pig he had bought dove overboard and "swam like a porpoise" for shore, a half mile away. Haskell thought he'd never see the pig again, but a farmer on shore returned the animal.

"Sunday, Sept. 9, 1928: Still outside the sea buoy and tacking. About 9 a.m., a white United Fruit vessel steamed by us towards the inner harbor. It was none other than the SAN GIL upon which I made my first three voyages in the fall of 1926. They will be tied up at Long Wharf in an hour—we may be here for days."

In the late 1930s, CRESSY was towed to Medomak, where she became part of a lobster pound. Much deteriorated (right) she remains there today. Top photo courtesy of the Maine Maritime Museum

Seaver, who went on to serve in the merchant marine, wrote that after tacking outside Boston Harbor for hours, a tug came alongside and "towed" CRESSY in. In fact, a north wind sprang up and CRESSY was abeam of the tug most of the way.

His final journal entry:

"Sept. 10, 1928: Worked all morning with impatience to be off ashore, home. Furled the topsails for the last time and, to celebrate the moment, slid down the halyards in one glorious hand-burning swoop.

"After a deal of paper shuffling, I received a discharge marked VG in the little boxes after conduct and ability. Also $22. I went home feeling mighty salty."

Steve Cartwright *is a freelance writer based in Waldoboro. He writes regularly for Island Institute publications.*

▌February 25, 1938	▌March 21, 1938	▌1960–1980	▌May, 2002
The *Boston Traveler* reports that "funeral services" for the **CRESSY**, "once queen of the seas," were being planned.	The *Boston Herald* reports the **CRESSY**— stripped of masts and fittings—was to be towed from Boston Harbor that day to become a "lobster storage boat" at Bernard Zahn's business in Medomak (Bremen), Maine.	Various pieces of the **CRESSY** are carried away, many of them to the Bath Marine Museum, later re-named Maine Maritime Museum.	The crumbling hulk of the **CRESSY** is, even in ruins, an awe-inspiring sight.

Washing Ashore

AND FINDING A NICHE IN COREA

MURIEL L. HENDRIX

From a small outboard (right), Jean Symonds worked her way up to a 33-footer.

Jean Symonds, who moved to Corea from Washington, D.C., in 1970, when she was in her early 30s, says she always felt she must have provided a lot of entertainment for the people in the village while she learned to fish for lobsters. She believes she must have caused some frustrations, too, but nobody seemed to mind enough to encourage her to quit. Instead, they gave her a lot of help. "This is an unusual place," she says, talking in her home which overlooks Corea Harbor. "There's a lot of support for new people who come in, a lot of camaraderie."

In 1971, when Symonds first expressed an interest in fishing, her next door neighbor, Clifford Young, now deceased, gave her five wooden traps, and another fisherman down the road contributed five buoys. After neighborhood kids taught her how to rig them, she used a rowboat to set the traps. "Most of the people probably thought this was just a passing fancy," she says, but Colby Young, who was about 33 at the time, recalls, "No one thought too much about it. They just felt she should go for it."

Symonds and "Dodie" Kemske ran Harbor Grocery for eight years.

Symonds, who in Young's words, "washed ashore in Corea," which has about 140 year-round residents, feels she was meant to live there. She and Dorothy ("Dodie") Kemske, who was her partner for 40 years until Kemske's death two years ago, were vacationing in the Belgrade Lakes area when they decided to investigate an ad saying a lighthouse was for sale in Prospect Harbor. The ad turned out to be a misrepresentation, but when Symonds and Kemske left Prospect Harbor and drove the long way back to Route 1, they noticed the road to Corea and decided to explore. Reaching the village and passing the church, they saw a For Sale sign on some house lots. They bought one on the spot, and the next summer, they built a cottage. "I was supposed to go to Boston College that fall to begin a doctorate," Symonds says, "but I couldn't leave Maine." The doctorate had to wait for several years.

When Symonds and Kemske landed in Corea, Kemske, 12 years older, was a retired army colonel, but Symonds, who had taught nursing at Georgetown University, needed to find a new way to make a living. "I thought the village could use a store," she says, "so we just did it." They spent the fall and winter visiting wholesalers and remodeling a fish house on a wharf which is part of property they later bought. Kemske, who Symonds says was much neater and better organized than she, took an accounting course at a local high school so she could keep the books for the business. "She would always think I was kind of crazy with all my ideas," Symonds says, "but she always helped me live my dream."

Kemske continued this kind of support when Symonds took up fishing. She learned how to knit bait bags, and when Symonds smashed her hand on a ledge while catching rocks to weigh down her traps, Kemske made the ultimate sacrifice. She filled the bags.

"It looked like I wouldn't be able to get the traps in that summer," Symonds says, "and I was so upset. I wanted to get on board. I figured out that with the hauler, I could do it, if I didn't have to fill the bait bags. Poor Dodie, she filled them every night for weeks."

They ran the store, Harbor Grocery, for eight years, until Symonds' foster mother moved in with them and needed care. The grocery quickly provided a popular gathering spot for village residents of all ages. Fishermen kept their coffee mugs on nails above the coffee pot; young people hung around after school. The constant exposure to talk about fishing and seeing everyone go out gave Symonds the itch to join in. "I looked out and realized that everybody, husbands, wives and kids, was fishing," she says. "I hate to be indoors; I wanted to be out there, too."

She put in her five traps—not in the immediate harbor, which was by tradition reserved for kids—but just outside. "I rowed out every day to pull them," she says. "I couldn't wait. I know it's not original to say this—everybody feels it—but you never know what's going to come up. It's like a Christmas present every time. There may be nothing, or all sorts of critters."

Her most memorable pull came the day she hauled in two traps and in the second, found an oversized lobster wearing fishermen's gloves. "A fisherman had got it in his trap, banded it, put on the gloves and planted it in my trap," she explains. "Of course I had to get on the radio. 'Oh, it's going to be a cold winter,' they said. 'Jean's got a lobster with gloves on.'"

During her second year, she put in about 35 traps, still pulling by hand. Then it was 75, then 150, and now, 500, including 100 brand new ones. "It became like a disease," she admits. "I wanted more traps, a bigger boat." She bought a little motor for the rowboat, graduated to a skiff with a motor, still hauling by hand, then an inboard 21-foot boat with a hauler. In 1980, she had a 30-foot boat built by Young Brothers Boat in Corea and used it for 19 years. She financed that boat, the FINEST KIND, with money she had inherited from her birth mother, whose initial reaction to her desire to fish had been that she would "ruin her skin." "Her spirit must have been turning in her grave," Symonds says, laughing.

Several years ago, Symonds switched to wire traps, and in 2000, she replaced FINEST KIND with a 33-foot diesel built by Young Brothers and finished by Mike Light. FINEST KIND II is outfitted with radar and all sorts of modern electronics, another dream come true.

Over the years, while Symonds persevered, learning by trial and error, many fishermen lent a helping hand when she needed it. One taught her how to build wooden traps. Some told her productive places to set her traps. "Ernest Woodward (now deceased) told me early on, 'If you put a couple right here,' near a particular ledge, it would be a good place," she says. "I've never missed a year putting in there and he was right." Once, when a storm came in too quickly for her to haul her 50 traps with the small skiff, Colby Young went out in his boat and pulled them for her. "He re-set them several days later," she says, "putting in rocks again to weigh them down."

After she had been fishing for two seasons, the manager of Corea Lobster Cooperative asked her why didn't she apply to join. She was skeptical, but applied anyway and was accepted. "That made me feel more like I belonged," she says.

A couple of times, fishermen have helped her find her way home when she was caught in fog and became disoriented. "Everyone knows fog has never been my friend," she admits. "I won't start out, and I won't stay out in the fog, even though with my new boat I could navigate home." Her closest call came in 1998 when the depth finder on FINEST KIND stopped working and she couldn't find her way out of a cove. "One of the fishermen was nearby," she says. "He told me to stay put, and he'd be right back, so I figured nobody would know. But I drifted and had to go on the radio, and then everybody knew Jean was lost again." But as Colby Young makes clear, nobody minded because it had happened to them sometime in the past. "In the days gone by before electronics, you had to navigate by the seat of your pants, and it was easy to get turned around," he says. "Jean does all right."

Young emphasizes that the helping hasn't been a one-way street. "Jean does a lot for the community," he notes. "Any-

Young Brothers Boat, in Corea, built FINEST KIND II for Symonds in the 1980s.

body needs anything and she's aware of it, she's on the scene—medical, personal, financial or just to talk—she's there." She also has volunteered regularly at Dorcas Library in Prospect Harbor and at Mabel Wadsworth Women's Health Center in Bangor.

One of Symonds and Kemske's greatest gifts to the community has been to ensure that after they both died, the wharf on their property would pass on to a fisherman. To accomplish this, they divided the property and arranged shared ownership of the section with the wharf with Dan Rodgers, a 24-year-old local fisherman.

"They started letting me use the wharf when I was a kid," Rodgers says.

"They didn't like seeing me have to lug my traps back to my parents' house. Other wharves in the harbor have been sold to non-fishing folks and are gone," he adds. "No one who's fishing could afford to buy them." Now, he and Symonds share space on the wharf for their traps, and they contributed equally when it needed to be rebuilt.

"It's one of the things you don't see happen very much in this day and age—no strings attached," says Dan's father, Dwight. "It was done in the true sense of generosity. Jean's character is best expressed through that action. She has been a very generous person over the years to a whole number of people."

The majority of women who fish have grown up in fishing families, but Symonds had zero experience when she first moved to Corea. Even so, she wasn't as clueless as poet Amy Clampitt, who while visiting Symonds, looked at the boats in the harbor and blurted out, "Oh I think it's

wonderful that everybody parks facing in the same direction."

Symonds spent her youth on a farm in Reading, Massachusetts, where the only body of water was a small pond. Working on the farm, which was owned by her foster mother and father, she developed a strong work ethic that spurred her to earn a diploma as a registered nurse, a BS at Boston College with a major in nursing and minor in English Literature, and to enter the Army Nurse Corps, where she helped teach medical skills to members of Special Forces teams. Later, she earned a Masters in Nursing at Boston University and taught at Georgetown University for five years. After moving to Corea, she used part of several summers to complete a PhD in Higher Education Administration at Vanderbilt University. For 15 years, she taught Women's Studies and nursing at the University of Maine at Orono, retiring in 1999.

At no time, before she moved to Corea, did she gain any expertise about running and navigating a boat, or how to bait, set and pull lobster traps, much less how to take marks so she could find the traps again. "I lost a lot of traps in the early years," she says. But she was determined. Colby Young, who himself has been "in, around, over or under the water for 51 years," observes, "Jean's a very smart lady who picks things up quick. Once she's made up her mind she's gonna do something, she does real well."

Although Symonds, now 68, wishes she didn't have to ask for help, she generally accepts her limitations. "I don't deal with engines and motors," she says, "but it is

frustrating not to know how to fix things, or sometimes, like when I can't get a bolt free or something like that, not to be a strong as a man." In the fall, Kenneth King, a military retiree who settled in the Corea area, helps her bring in her traps and hoist them onto the wharf.

Symonds has always fished alone. "I haven't wanted to have a stern man," she says, "because it's so nice to go at my own pace, and at my age, not have to push myself beyond what I'm capable of. With a stern man, I would feel like I'd really have to work harder to make sure he would get a good living. But if I did have help, I could shift my traps more and get more done in a day. I don't really want to, but may have to sometime."

There are days, she admits, when it's an effort to go out, particularly after being ashore for awhile due to bad weather. "It can be hard to re-start and face it again," she says, "but that's rare. It may sound childish, but there's not a Spring that's gone by when I haven't taken my first ride on the boat and just screamed with joy once I'm out in the harbor on my own.

"I often think, how many people in this world have the opportunity to see what I do? To watch the sun spill out on the horizon, see the beautiful colors everywhere, the boats coming out with their lights on and people coming by and saying hello. It's a wonderful way of life."

*Some of the information for this story was taken from an interview conducted by **Robert Bayer** and **Cathy Billings** for The Lobster Institute's Oral History Project. Photographs courtesy of **Jean Symonds**.*

TIED

After 72 years,
the elegant
DOUBLE EAGLE
may have outlived
her fishery

BEN NEAL

The gray sardine carrier DOUBLE EAGLE can be seen most often on winter days inconspicuously tied to the Fish Pier in Rockland. Her name boards are off, and being double-ended, she has no stern on which to paint a name or port. She is quiet and cold, snow hiding her workaday but sound wooden deck. Uncluttered and bare, she is clear of the salt bags, herring scale collectors and baskets that would give away her occupation. But the strength of the deck fittings, the large midships hatch, and most of all the sweep of her sheer identify her as a classic Maine herring carrier. Rising up in the bow, as she is riding light at the pier, this is an archetypal working vessel of the coastal waters of the northern Gulf of Maine, designed to take a thousand bushels of herring from the weirs and seines that used to be scattered along the coast and bring them to market or factory.

UP

Unloading herring for lobster bait in Vinalhaven

From Gloucester to Nova Scotia DOUBLE EAGLE has ranged, transporting tens of million of pounds of herring over a 72-year working life. Despite her age, she is sound and updated through and through, waiting only for spring to work another season.

The early riser on Vinalhaven or Matinicus could catch the vessel unloading bait herring to lobster co-ops or directly into waiting lobster boats. She will have slipped in under cover of darkness, coming from a midnight seine set. Catching and selling herring for lobster bait and sardines has long been a cooperative venture,

involving both a catcher boat and a carrier. The purse seiner NIGHT OWL of Vinalhaven and DOUBLE EAGLE have been fishing together for these elusive little fish for a decade, with the owners and captains going back together almost another decade on other vessels. They fish for herring in the dark of night, when the little fish rise up to the surface and congregate in tight schools, and now they sell all their catch fresh the following morning directly to local lobstermen and fishermen's co-ops. The herring fishery in the midcoast area where these boats operate is primarily a summer and fall fishery, with the boats relying on the lobster season for providing most of their year's income.

Maine harbors and coves have known many such carriers over the years, most of which have faded away with the canneries, and only few of them survive today in working trim. The large and graceful PAULINE, the JACOB PIKE and her lost sister MARY ANN and the sail carrier SYLVINA BEAL (which was converted to power and then, after a long fishing life, went back to sail as a passenger carrying vessel) are but a few of the many herring carriers that worked the coves, islands and factories.

From transporting herring to a hundred now-gone canneries to bringing in a daily bait supply for upwards of 300 island lobstermen, DOUBLE EAGLE has adapted, and manages to continue the same work she has for 72 years, carrying a portion of Maine's largest fishery to market. However, this way of life may be changing, and the venerable wooden boat may outlast her function, facing decreasing market share, competition dominated by larger vessels, changing regulations and a potentially decreasing coastal stock of herring, the foundation of not only the carrier's work, but also of the entire coastal ecosystem.

From the beginning of the sardine industry at the time of the Franco-Prussian War of 1870 (which spurred the development of North American herring packing, due to the wartime disruption of European production) until about 1910, herring were transported by small, sailing, "carry-away" boats. Generally each cannery also provided for a steam tug, to tow these sloops and schooners in times of no wind. After 1910, the sailing vessels gradually began installing gas auxiliaries. Next came power vessels with auxiliary sails, and by 1920 sail had all but disappeared from the carrier fleet. There was an attendant increase in carrying capacity from around 10-15 hogsheads (12, 400 to 18,600 pounds; the hogshead, a traditional barrel measure of 1,240 pounds, and the bushel are still in use as measures in the herring industry), to the larger carriers of the 1940s able to pack over 100 hogsheads. Catching methods also evolved, from the brush weirs of before World War I to the stop-seine fishery that saw a dory moored in virtually every cove along the coast, marking the spot for the owner should the fish come into that cove, to the purse-seine fishery that developed after World War II, taking the harvest further to sea in pursuit of the fish, and recently to mid-water trawling. The carriers serviced all these methods but the last, and the requirements remained much the same, for an able and seakindly vessel capable of a good turn of speed while loaded, small and agile enough to duck into any of a thousand

Nakomis Nelson

coves along the coast that might have a shut-off, and stout enough to take the knocks that working close to shore in the dark of night was sure to produce. The evolution of the type from sailing vessels remained evident in the long, low and slippery, often beautiful hulls. Even though they worked long hours, the vessels were spared the rigors of working heavy fishing gear, and with the nearly yacht-like maintenance that many long-time masters and mates lavished on them, many of the vessels enjoyed long lives.

DOUBLE EAGLE was built by Charles Ingalls in 1929 at East Machias, Maine, for the North Lubec Manufacturing and Canning Company. In the early years she was used both as a sardine carrier and a general freight boat. As a freight boat, it is likely that she carried her house forward of the hatches, in the manner of a tug, and had it relocated aft when the vessel was used only for carrying fish. Her launch was covered in July of 1929 by the *Eastport Sentinel*, which described the vessel as "sturdily built of white oak and yellow birch, with a deep hold." She was approximately 65 feet in length, with a 20-foot beam, and powered by a 75-horsepower Fairbanks-Morse crude oil engine. Now, two rebuilds and innumerable repairs later, she has little of this original wood in her, and has with age become longer, beamier and more powerful.

The vessel took her name from the trademark of the company, which featured

a two-headed eagle, reminiscent of the symbol of the Hanseatic League of the Baltic, another group that made its fortune on herring. The Double Eagle label and brand of sardines was the oldest sardine brand name in continuous use in Maine, first used when The Lubec Packing Company was incorporated in 1880, and still in use 110 years later when the final version of the company was dissolved. Although the company had changed its incorporation, factories and even name several times, as was common in the economically volatile packing business, when it finally broke up for good in 1990, it was still run by members of the same Lawrence family that originally incorporated it, and was still packing fish marked with the double eagle. The last North Lubec Packing Company factory to be closed was the Rockland plant on Tilson wharf, which ceased operation in 1990, seven years

EAGLE BRAND
AMERICAN SARDINES IN MUSTARD SAUCE

REG. U.S. PAT. OFF.

PACKED BY
NORTH LUBEC MANUFACTURING & CANNING CO..
FACTORIES - NORTH LUBEC. STONINGTON & ROCKLAND, ME.
THIS MUSTARD SAUCE IS MADE FROM SELECT
MUSTARD SEED, VINEGAR, CAYENNE PEPPER,
SALT, AND COLORED WITH TURMERIC.
CONTENTS 3¼ AVOIR OZS.
PAT NOV 3, 1903. AM CAN CO, 32 A-14

DOUBLE EAGLE in Boothbay, 1968

before the 1997 closing of the Conners Bros.-Port Clyde Canning Company factory left the city of Rockland without a sardine factory for the first time in almost a century.

Built following the years of expansion in the late 1920s, and launched just in time for the stock market crash of 1929 and the Great Depression, DOUBLE EAGLE survived the subsequent consolidation of the Lubec Packing Company. She worked through the lean years of the 1930s as one of four company boats delivering fish to the two Lubec plants, named the "Battle Axe" and the "Penny Catcher," as well as to a new plant in Rockland. Things improved with the war years, which were boom times for the fish packing business when they could find enough labor at home to work the plants. The postwar years brought back both labor and market. Many carriers were built or improved following the war, and in 1949 DOUBLE EAGLE was sent east to the shores of St. Mary's Bay, to the A.F. Theriault yard in Meteghan, Nova Scotia, to be rebuilt. She returned a new vessel, having been cut in half and lengthened out twelve feet, and fitted with a new double-ended stern where she had previously carried the more traditional "fantail" shape. Capacity was increased to 80 hogsheads, or 1,330 bushels. Around this time a new 120-hp Buda diesel engine was also fitted. After the refit she returned to

During the rebuild in Rockland, 1991

Penobscot Bay to service the expanding seine fleet, generally running fish to Rockland with DeCosta Pine as master, and Carleton Winchenbach as mate. Making things easier on deck was a revolutionary new fish pump, now a standard feature on fishing vessels. DOUBLE EAGLE was one of first Maine herring boats to be fitted with this labor-saving device, greatly speeding up the loading process. Prior to this all the fish was brought on board by hand, one dip at a time, using a brail net.

Sardine consumption and herring packing declined throughout the 1960s and 70s. Most of the factories were operating only sporadically and many were closing their doors for good. Herring were scarce, and the industry that had once employed thousands, packing millions of cans of fish in dozens of factories from Eastport to Portland, was in serious decline. With the idling of the Rockland plant in 1984, DOUBLE EAGLE was out of a job, and was sold to an owner in New Harbor for use in the "pogy" trade, carrying menhaden to oil reduction plants and foreign vessels. Hard used in this marginal fishery, she found herself beginning her sixth decade tied to a wharf with her keel in the mud. With parts of her rail gone, deck gear deteriorated, the after mast leaning, a rotten house and a patched and leaky deck over the forecastle, like many other wooden carriers the vessel could well have found her final berth.

However, the boat fell under the discerning eye of Geno Scalzo, a traditional boatbuilder of Owls Head. Through the surface deterioration, he saw a seakindly and stout working hull, and recommended the vessel to current owner Glen Lawrence, oddly enough of the same name (no relation) as her original owner.

Glen Lawrence, owner, rebuilder and operator

Together they purchased the vessel, brought her to the North End Shipyard in Rockland, and over a period of nearly a year completely rebuilt her. This was no romantic notion—they wanted an economical and stout working boat, capable of working summer and winter, carrying 100,000 pounds of herring to market each day. At first intending only repairs, they found upon opening up the boat that more was required, and eventually stripped and refitted the entire vessel, in the end replacing the majority of the wood in the hull and overhauling all systems.

DOUBLE EAGLE was given a new start from the keel up, with 24 inches of fresh oak scarfed into the after end. Stout bilge stringers were fitted, increasing longitudinal strength, and steel floors were bolted down in the area of the fish hold.

Original hackmatack frames were mostly cut back to sound wood, and new white oak frames fitted between them. Deep within the vessel they came across wood labeled for the yard in Meteghan, Nova Scotia, where the vessel was last rebuilt, 42 years prior. The vessel was widened slightly, and the sheer brought up, especially in the bow. Where she had just rotting log rails before, substantial stanchions and bulwarks were installed. Eight tons of concrete ballast steadied the boat and provided the sole of the hold. Her relatively new GM 671 diesel was re-secured to new engine beds, a new wooden deck was laid, and a completely new and larger deckhouse was built. The only fiberglass used in the whole vessel was in the house roof and hatch cover. Topping it off was a dignified coat of gray paint and hand carved name boards. In late fall of 1991, she was ready for launch, better than new and with a new job waiting.

A test of the strength of the rebuilt vessel came right at the launch, when her stern was dropped a number of times onto the ground by the launching crane. No damage was incurred, and the launch went ahead, followed by a dance and celebration. DOUBLE EAGLE returned quickly to the working life, with Glen Lawrence understandably anxious to get the vessel back into carrying fish and earning money. Shortly after the launch he steamed south to Gloucester for the winter herring fishery, with many jobs being completed while he was underway, including replacing the vice-grips he was using for steering with a proper wheel. Another test came in 1993, when she was steaming through the night loaded with fish, and ran full bore up onto the Wooden Ball, about 10 miles south of Vinalhaven. Glen had just lain down for a rest, and left the helm with the young mate. Seven knots of speed and the momentum of 100,000 pounds of fish ran her hard onto the ledge, and she had to be hauled off in the morning, with Glen watching up forward for an inrush of water through damaged plank hood-ends. No water came, however, despite having lost some parts of the stem, and they finished their workday rounds of Matinicus, Vinalhaven and Rockland, unloaded all the fish, and then hauled out the boat. In doing the repairs, the strength of the boat was evident; in the course of the repairs Glen found that he had to make up though-bolts fully 38 inches long to reach through the stem.

DOUBLE EAGLE was once again fully employed, carrying fish for the canneries in Massachusetts Bay in the winters, and working a predominantly Maine island bait trade in the summers. Slipping in before dawn, she sold herring to lobster-

Winter fishing in the early 1990s

men on Frenchboro and Swan's Islands, Isle Au Haut and Deer Isle, Vinalhaven and Matinicus and points in between.

Today the herring business seems harder and harder to pursue, and Glen is uncertain what the coming season may bring.

The herring season has gone in recent years from being an open fishery, with few restrictions on when herring could be landed, to being open only a certain number of days each week, and closing altogether in the late fall. For small inshore boats like the NIGHT OWL and the DOUBLE EAGLE, not being able to go out on good nights hurts because it forces them to try on bad nights when they are allowed to fish. They also rely on markets that need to be supplied daily, and having closed days means that they cannot provide fresh product. It is inevitable that buyers will have to look to more reliable trucked bait, and a market may be lost. There is fear among the inshore fishermen that if this continues, then local small-boat herring fishing is going to be a thing of the past.

Glen is worried about the state of the coastal herring stock, and supports some of the limits that have led to the shutdowns. But he contends that the real problem is that ever-larger vessels are using trawl gear in the inshore area, and are altering the behavior and size of the herring schools, decreasing both the size and reproduction of the coastal stock. It's harder for inshore vessels such as himself and the NIGHT OWL, who rely on aggre-

gations of fish closer to the coast, to find the fish they need to operate. Not all regulators or fishermen agree that fishing with trawl nets has had this impact, but the issue of the effects of this gear on the herring stock has recently garnered additional attention from state regulatory agencies. Maine Department of Marine Resources Commissioner George LaPointe sent a letter last August to the Atlantic States Marine Fisheries Commission (which regulates herring fishing) noting that "there is here in Maine a growing concern about the effects of midwater trawling for Atlantic herring on the resource," and requesting "a thorough, unbiased review of the impact of midwater trawling and other fishing gear."

Large midwater trawl vessels operate legally in Maine waters, but some fishermen feel that these often out-of-state vessels are taking over what has been to date one of Maine's most traditional fisheries, conducted primarily by smaller, in-state vessels. It is no secret that coastal herring have decreased, as any older coastal or island fisherman can attest — but federal regulators contend that the herring resource is healthy and strong, just farther offshore. For Glen Lawrence and DOUBLE EAGLE it is far from an academic question, as access to the very resource, which has sustained the boat for seven decades, is threatened. Glen is concerned not only for himself and the boat but also for the health of the herring resource. "At this rate I'm not going to last a year, and I'm not too hopeful for the seals or the fish either."

Without the capacity or size to shift to another region or fishery when the

inshore herring quota is finished, DOUBLE EAGLE stays tied to the pier. She is unable to pursue the fishery on Georges Bank, as larger vessels can. So she waits, a purpose-built boat for a fishery that should have lasted forever. Herring fishing has changed in the past, and the canneries that used to be the mainstay for boats like the DOUBLE EAGLE are not likely to ever return. But with her sound backbone of oak, and with the long patience of a boat that has gone from boom times to the Great Depression, and from a mud berth through two rebuilds, she waits once more for the return of the shoals of herring that have long sustained generations of island and coastal residents.

---

*Thanks to **Geno Scalzo**, master shipwright of Owls Head, **John Gilman**, author of Masts and Masters, A Brief History of Sardine Carriers and Boatmen, and Canned, A History of the Sardine Industry, and to **Glen Lawrence**, owner and operator of DOUBLE EAGLE. Except where credited otherwise, all photos courtesy of **Glen Lawrence**.*

Summer Ice

Photographs by
GARY COMER

*Black and white photographs by
Donald MacMillian. Courtesy of
The Peary-MacMillan Arctic Museum
and Arctic Studies Center, Bowdoin College,
Brunswick, Maine.*

From the log of TURMOIL

July 10, 2001 *(facing page):*

Some of the icebergs are adrift in the
currents, and some are so massive that
they are aground in 900 feet of water
with another 300 feet of their white sails
still frozen in the air. We skirt the edges
of the ice field. Every quarter of an hour
or so there is the sharp report of the
sound like a rifle shot that brings us
quickly out of our rapture to look up
anxiously at the towering faces of ice.
Other pieces of ice groan and crack as
they uneasily shift their positions to gain
repose. Your life can seem relatively
insignificant here....

"Greenland," wrote artist-adventurer Rockwell Kent in 1931, "that small part of which is not buried under the eternal ice cap ... is a stark, bare, treeless land with naked rock predominating everywhere." While Kent's description reflects Greenland's bleakness, it doesn't do justice to the beauty one also encounters on and around this vast island. Its mountain glaciers and floating ice, moving as they melt in the high Arctic sun, are spectacular examples of powerful, dangerous natural forces at work. Ten percent of the icebergs in the entire North Atlantic originate in a single bay in West Greenland.

In July, 2001, the private expedition vessel TURMOIL ventured up Greenland's western shore. Impassible pack ice in Melville Bay forced TURMOIL to turn back on July 16 after a thousand-mile voyage up Greenland's west coast. Along the way the vessel's owner, Gary Comer, took the color photographs on these pages, and I kept the ship's log. Portions of that log appear along with the images, as well as a selection of archival photographs taken in the 1930s and 1940s by Donald MacMillan, who visited Greenland's west coast many times during his trips to the Arctic.

TURMOIL then headed across Baffin Bay and with the unprecedented rapid melting of the Arctic Ice Cap, she completed a crossing of the legendary Northwest Passage during the third week of August. TURMOIL thus became the first private, unassisted vessel to complete the Northwest passage in a single season in history. But that's another story.

— Philip Conkling

Maniitsoq (Sukkertoppen)

July 6, 2001: ...The present settlement of Maniitsoq was founded in 1781, having moved from an earlier 1755 location to be nearer to better fishing and whaling grounds. The town was originally known as Sukkertoppen (sugar-loaf) from the name of the mountain glacier overhead.... Greenland was disputed territory between Denmark and Norway. The dispute was finally settled at the World Court in the Hague in the 1930s.

Maine-based explorer Donald MacMillan visited the same area in the 1940s when it was still known by its Danish name. Summer snow and ice on the mountains was thick when he took this photograph, and a comparison of the two images hints at warming in the decades since then.

July 11, 2001: We chance a passage across iceberg alley to Qequerrtsuaq (literally, the "Big Island" or Disko Island to Europeans) which is by far the largest island off Greenland's west coast.... Once outside the harbor, we turn briefly south to take one last look at the calving grounds of the North Atlantic's icebergs and can't resist launching the shore boats for a few more photographs.... We pass the "Sydney Opera House," the "Blue Lagoon" and "Deep Throat," the latter two of which have graceful arches sculpted out by melting waters.... But mindful of their instability, we maintain a respectful distance although by the time we pass, these may be the most photographed pieces of ice in the western world.

Disko Bay (Qequerrtsuaq)

Aboard his schooner BOWDOIN, Donald MacMillan made a half-dozen visits to Disko Bay from the 1920s to the 1950s. Some scenes remain relatively unchanged today.

Kangaamiut (Sondrestrom Fiord)

July 8, 2001: We awake to another superlative day of bright sun and light winds. Just to the south of our anchorage behind Kangaamiut, the line of fog has remained stationary. Over breakfast we discuss the atmospheric dynamics of the fog. With a light southerly breeze, you would assume that the fog bank would be pushed north to envelop the boat at anchor in this little bay, but it stays in place a mile to the south.... perhaps the influence of the fiords changes the dew point enough to condense water vapor from the air, but this cannot explain the distance the fog extends out into Davis Strait. Checking the weather chart, it appears we are on the southern edge of a high pressure cell which has drifted slowly over Davis Strait.... That might be part of an explanation.

Ililussat (Jakobshavn)

July 10, 2001: The path winds through tundra wildflowers up onto one rocky shelf after another to the final cairn where spread below is a unique Arctic creation. The scene spreads out beneath our feet of a giant ice sheet inclined toward Disko Bay off to our right. Back around the corner to our left is a lobe of the fiord that is ice free but blocked by the passage of the massive flanks of the ice. Out in the middle of the ice sheet, massive pressure ridges build a hundred feet high, stacked like frozen contorted waves with their galloping white caps pointed to the sky. We have read that this ice sheet moves at the astonishing rate of 100 feet a day.... We have heard that periodically the water in the open lobe of the fiord that has backed up for weeks or months surges under the ice and breaks free of its ice dam to send a little tsunami out into the bay large enough to swamp the harbor and cause real havoc. The night air is clear and warm and disturbingly still. As a result the winged furies are in their element and with our aromatic signatures enveloping us, we advertise ourselves as one of the few available feeding stations. As a result we do not tarry for long at this corner of heavenly creation. But to have seen this spectacle of the birth canal of icebergs, if only for an instant, is to satisfy the imagination for a lifetime.

MacMillan and the BOWDOIN also visited Jakobshavn, anchoring amid ice cakes off the village in 1939.

Melville Bay

July 16, 2001: The early morning light collects in pure pools of silver across the eastern edge of Melville Bay. Not a cat's paw of wind disturbs the surface of the sea in a breathless inhalation of dawn. The vaporous eastern sky is the palest ion blue while the horizon's clouds to the west merge imperceptively with the shimmering edge of the water. No distinct line separates sea, air, ice or light where the curvature of the heaven meets the arc of the circumpolar sea. It's as if the elements shift from one semi-solid state to another. Nothing here is fixed; nothing seems certain.

We've gone as far as we can go for the time being on our northerly course and turn west paralleling the broad curve of the land. To add to the mystery and eeriness of the place, long luminous green tendrils of some kind of life form begin appearing in the water a meter or so deep looking pale and shining at the same time. These can only be streaks of plankton, but this thought raises as many new questions as answers. Why they are arranged in long lines; what pale fire lights these numinous streaks?

.... There is room for Turmoil to maneuver, so onward through the ice we press and pry. At one point our bow wave brushes up against a piece of ice the size of a backyard swimming pool. As the wave disturbs the ice, it breaks into a few pieces and then it dematerializes. It simply becomes water before our wondering eyes.

Now that we have arrived at the pack ice north of the 75th parallel, life has suddenly exploded around us. Flocks of murres and dovekies fly by as if they were pellets shot from a shotgun. Fulmers tilt past, dipping one wing and then the other to navigate the sinuous ice margins....

The further we twist and turn our way into the ice flows, the more abundant becomes the marine life. The base of the food chain here is a brown algae that attaches to the bottom of the ice, photosynthesizing through the transluscent light. Various zooplankton graze on this food supply and become food for larger shrimp like creatures which feed the fish and seabirds which feed the seals and whales. The idea that the ice is lifeless is a temperate zone concept that is turned on its head here in the Arctic.

And what a food chain it is! Murres and dovekies in their millions explode into view. Estimates of the number of dovekies in Baffin Bay run as high as 30 million, an inconceivable number calling to mind the general ecological rule of thumb that as one proceeds toward the poles, the fewer the species, but the greater their abundance. But when viewing a single small dovekie feeding in these teeming waters what does such an abstract rule or number mean? On its way back to its mate at a single rock crevice nest, a dovekie is not be some numberless creature, but a particular bird that will return to its individual nest as true as an arrow flies.What do we really know about their life?

As we proceed on our meandering northwesterly course, a dilimma stares us in the face. If we assume that the satellite ice map of yesterday showing the extent of the pack ice 100 miles across our course has somehow greatly dissipated, we might be able to traverse Melville Bay at 5-6 knots to reach Cape York in another day of strain on the crew and vessel. Another 75 miles beyond Cape York is Thule, our ultimate goal.... Assuming the weather does not change to cause a closing of the ice behind us and that the fog does not creep in around us to make navigation in the dense ice filed impossible; we could still get nearly to Thule without ever getting there. We could conceivably get to within 10 miles of Thule or even a mile and not be able to land on shore.

Nevertheless, we steam on, winding through the magnifiscent narrow channels flaked by icebergs and shoals of pancake and brash ice at half speed, not quite willing to come this close to our end, the legendary destination of Thule, and just let it go.... The sun burns hazy holes through the high cloud cover. The wind inhales deeply and holds its breath. Every sensation is full and rounded. If only this would never end.

Late in the afternoon a final set of satellite ice maps seals the decision we had all silently reached earlier. TURMOIL nudges up to a floating ice pan and shudders to a halt. Slowly, painfully she backs down and thrusts her bow around in a broad arc. We rejoin the vessel and the crew, load the shore boat back on the deck and facing aft, begin retracing our course to the south.

THE QUODDY REGION
Outer Bay of Fundy

THE LARGEST SARDINE FACTORY IN THE WORLD, CHAMCOOK, N.B.

A MARINE OASIS IN DECLINE

JANICE HARVEY

I n the Quoddy Region in the outer Bay of Fundy, ocean currents and circulation patterns, high tides and upwellings support high concentrations of primary and secondary producers, and a short, energy-efficient pelagic food chain (diatoms—krill—fish—birds—mammals). Abundant "lower order" species attract a wide range of predators from near and far to feed or nurse their young. Added to this abundant food supply are the diverse underwater, riverine and terrestrial habitats that provide breeding, spawning, nursing, feeding, foraging, hiding and resting conditions for myriad species. Together, these conditions create a hotspot of species diversity and productivity.

Throughout the world, there are a few marine regions of such importance to a diverse array of species that they warrant special attention. The Quoddy-Bay of Fundy region is one of them.

There are a few particularly "hot" spots within the Quoddy region, critical habitats because they are used by many species at once. Head Harbour and L'Etete Passages and their approaches (within the West Isles archipelago), the eastern Grand Manan archipelago including Machias Seal Island to the south, The Wolves islands and Maces Bay at the northerly reach of the Quoddy Region—all support a diversity of species inter-acting among and with each other as predator and prey, and finding refuge and nursery areas.

Predictably, this biological oasis has over the centuries become fully utilized by humans. For thousands of years, the Passamaquoddy people and their ancestors lived, fished, hunted and cultivated land in the Quoddy region. Archeologists have called their distinct life style the "Quoddy Tradition" (2200-350 B.P.), differing from that of neighboring tribes by their particularly diverse utilization of marine species. In the Algonkian language, "Passamaquoddy" denotes a "bay full of pollock" and "fishers of pollock."

Over the 200 years since permanent European settlement in the late 18th century, humans as top predators and developers increased in number and efficiency. Many marine, avian and terrestrial resources became heavily exploited through fishing, hunting and lumbering. Numerous sawmills, pulp and paper mills, tanneries, fish processing and canning industries, cotton mills, power plants and eventually intensive finfish aquaculture, were established here, each spewing effluent and debris into rivers and bays virtually unchecked until the last 30 years (aquaculture in the region is just now coming

"WORLD'S LARGEST LOBSTER POUND, DEER ISLAND, N. B.
Owned And Operated By Conley's Lobsters Ltd., St. Andrews, N. B."

under environmental regulation). Dozens of dams became permanent features on rivers, tributaries and lakes in the Quoddy watershed. Species depletion and habitat degradation and loss have followed in lockstep.

In the 1960s, groundfish stocks collapsed in Passamaquoddy Bay, an area where pollock were once so abundant they were seined in nets. Despite a de facto moratorium on fishing effort ever since, as well as reductions in pollution loadings from pulp and saw mills, those stocks have not recovered. What has happened to undermine that system's restoration capacity? Has the bay undergone "ecological simplification," where the intricate interrelationship of species, habitats, food supply and reproductive conditions has been fundamentally compromised?

The Conservation Council of New Brunswick set out to answer these questions through a research project launched in the fall of 2000. The project proceeded on the assumption that natural systems respond to external impacts at varying scales and time frames, and it is only over the long term that major ecosystem changes or shifts may be evident. Investigators set the study area as the greater Quoddy region, and compiled archeological, historic and recent data in an effort to understand how current relationships between and among species, and between species and habitats, compare with such relationships 100 and 200 years ago, and even before Europeans settled the region.

Despite limitations in data (availability, comparability, lack of long-term monitoring, etc.), the investigators were able to identify some very troubling trends in the Quoddy region, beginning 200 years ago.

FOOD WEB ALTERATION

Through over-harvesting of fish, birds and mammals that began in the 19th century, and a predictable shift of harvesting effort from the top of the food web towards the bottom, humans have significantly altered the original food web structure in the region. By 1900, many top predator populations were in trouble. Several bird and marine mammal species had been decimated. Atlantic salmon and other migratory fish were blocked from upriver spawning grounds, causing population declines.

Also by 1900, the first sign of overexploitation of large fish was apparent —shifts in size distribution. The size of cod and pollock declined sharply, and the herring fishery shifted from large adults to medium stringers and eventually to small sardines. Lobster also shifted down-

ward in size, from many to only a couple of pounds. The second sign—drop in abundance—came by the 1970s, as groundfish and herring catches declined. Dogfish, hake and small groundfish such as sculpins increased in abundance and came to dominate the food web niches formerly occupied by large groundfish.

As commercially popular large fish declined, fishing effort shifted to species lower on the food chain. In recent decades, new fisheries for crabs, sea urchins and rockweed have been developed, while traditional fisheries for periwinkles, scallops and lobsters have intensified. There is also interest in sea cucumber, mussel and krill fisheries. Daniel Pauley calls this trend towards "fishing down the food web" a global pathology that feeds on itself. Since lower trophic level species are important prey for higher predators, or important habitat as in the case of rockweed, such harvesting could well undermine the recovery prospects for the higher species, hastening the total collapse of the ecosystem.

Planktonic species have demonstrated changes as well. While total primary production in the Quoddy ecosystem may not have declined over the past century (the data only cover the last 70 years or so), the occurrence and volume of phytoplankton species less edible to marine animals, and toxic species, have increased. While the effects of toxic algae on species higher on the food web (including humans) are known, the consequences of changes in food quality and quantity for zooplankton and higher level species are not.

In sum, species composition and abundance, dominance patterns and food-web structure of the marine ecosystem in the Quoddy region have been changed over the past 200 years. Major shifts include the loss or decline of large predatory species, increasing dominance of commercially less important and smaller species and an overall increase in opportunistic, generalist (rather than specialist) species. These shifts in species composition and dominance have resulted in a severe alteration of the entire food web, likely influencing predator-prey and competitive relationships among the species. In response, fishing effort has shifted lower and lower on the food chain, potentially fueling a continual downward spiral.

NUTRIENT LOADING

Coastal and estuarine waters are the most heavily fertilized environments in the world. Nutrient sources include sewage, agricultural runoff, aquaculture, municipal runoff, organic discharges (e.g. food processing plants, pulp mills), atmospheric deposition from the burning of fossil fuels. The over-enrichment of coastal waters with nitrogen and phosphorus has severe consequences, such as a decline in species diversity, decrease in light availability, increase in harmful algal blooms, increase in fast-growing annual macroalgae (e.g., green algae), decrease in dissolved oxygen, and loss and degradation of long-lived seagrass, kelp and coral reef communities and their associated animal and plant life.

A recent survey of 138 estuaries in the United States identified the St. Croix River-Cobscook Bay area in the inner Quoddy region as one of 44 estuaries with the highest indications of eutrophication —smothering of animal life by dense plant growth which uses up all dissolved oxygen in the water—due to nutrient loading. Conditions were expected to worsen by 2020. The most visible symptoms were the occurrence of harmful and toxic algal blooms and blooms of the annual green seaweeds.

Even so, elevated nutrient levels are hard to detect in the Quoddy region, which has naturally high levels of nutrients due to its tidal upwellings. There are a few exceptions—the L'Etang Inlet, which receives effluent from a pulp mill; Blacks Harbour, which receives effluent from a large fish cannery and fertilizer plant; and areas near salmon aquaculture sites. Municipal sewage outflows are also problem areas.

What isn't clear is whether the low background oxygen level in sediments in Passamaquoddy Bay is historically "normal" because of naturally high nutrients in the water, or whether it has diminished over the past 150 years as a result of loadings of organic sediments—materials that decompose over time, and in doing so use up oxygen needed by aquatic animals.

The sawmill industry of the 19th century was huge, with several mills on every stream dumping wood debris directly into the water. In the early 20th century three pulp mills came on line, adding massive amounts of sediments to receiving waters until the mid-to-late 1970s. Over 60 years, one pulp mill spewed three million metric tons of suspended solids into the St. Croix River. These discharges changed the bottom in every river and stream on which they sat. Most of them drain into Passamaquoddy Bay, which is known to circulate and settle out sediments, rather than flush them into more open adjacent waters.

It is possible that low oxygen in Passamaquoddy sediments is largely human-induced, over a time scale of 200 years. If this is the case, then the process may be ongoing as more contaminants are added from land runoff and net-pen aquaculture operations. It begs the question: where on the enrichment-eutrophication gradient is Passamaquoddy Bay, and when might a threshold be reached, beyond which the system collapses, losing its capability to support animal life? Part of the answer to the question of why groundfish have not recovered in Passamaquoddy Bay may be linked to gradual changes that have taken place in bottom-dwelling creatures at the base of the food web.

HABITAT LOSS AND DEGRADATION

The first dams were built on the St. Croix River in 1793. Remarkably, they had fishways. Many subsequent dams did not, and in the 1860s residents began to be concerned about the disappearance of salmon and gaspereau from the watershed. By

1909, salmon were nearly extirpated from the St. Croix. By the 1960s toxic water conditions from a pulp mill and bacterial pollution from sewage began killing fish. A river survey found sludge deposits seven feet deep in the St. Croix, comprised of coal ash, sawdust, wood chips, bark and sunken logs. Improvements in pollution and fish passage through the 1970s and 1980s had some success especially for gaspereau (alewives), but unilateral decisions by the State of Maine to block gaspereau first at Vanceboro (1987), then at Grand Falls (1991), and finally at Woodland (1995), caused the populations to crash once again.

Such is the history of most of the streams and rivers flowing into the Quoddy Region. Since these freshwater systems are integral to estuarine and coastal marine systems, the loss of anadromous fish from river habitat destruction or pollution has a ripple effect outward. As technology increased both the range and impact of human activity, direct impacts moved outward from the easily accessible rivers to the coast and islands. Draining wetlands, disturbance of nesting islands, bottom trawling, dragging and dredging, waste dumping, net-pen aquaculture, destruction of habitat-building species (rockweed, kelp, eelgrass, mussels), sediment loading, noise, light and smell pollution (acoustic harassments, artificial lights, fish and food wastes in aquaculture and fish processing plants) and interfering with marine mammals (ship collisions, fishing gear entanglement, increasing boat traffic)—all of these disturbances have altered, degraded, diminished or destroyed habi-tat throughout the Quoddy region over the past 200 years. Such impacts have severe consequences on the extent and quality of habitat for reproduction, feeding and foraging, refuge from predators and simply living.

OTHER FACTORS

There are other things going on in the system as well. Toxic loadings have been a factor over time, but since pollution controls were introduced beginning in the 1970s, levels of most toxins, such as DDT and PCBs, have decreased. The exception is PAHs, which remain very high in the St. Croix estuary. Mercury is also a concern and new monitoring is underway to quantify this. Both pollutants are persistent and extremely harmful to animal species, yet no studies have assessed impacts on populations from exposures to these substances.

A recent U.S. study suggests the bottom of Passamquoddy Bay is sinking approximately eight millimeters per year, resulting in a high degree of coastal erosion. The oldest prehistoric shell middens in Passamaquoddy Bay are around 3,000 years old, while to the east and west, mid-

New Brunswick, Canada's Picture Province . . . the old mill at St. George   Photo by 1

Cotton Mills and Falls at Milltown, N.B

dens are 6,000-7,000 years old. Surprisingly, scallop draggers found the remains of a coastal site from about 6,000 years ago offshore from Grand Manan and The Wolves. A border survey done in the summer of 2001 found the Canada-U.S. boundary markers placed on the bottom of the bay around 1900 had moved downwards as much as 30 to 60 cm since the last survey in 1966. Geologists are still puzzling about this phenomenon (they assume it is connected to the Oak Bay Fault which runs through the bay and up the St. Croix River to Oak Bay). With this unusual degree of shoreline erosion, we can assume that over the centuries, much intertidal habitat such as mudflat and salt marsh may have been lost.

Annual mean water temperature has also risen in the inner Quoddy region by 1.05 degrees C over the past 100 years. Changes in water temperature, both long and short term, are known to influence the use various species make of certain habitats or areas. In fish, temperature can affect growth and reproduction, food availability and distribution, and migration and depth distribution. Birds are also affected because for some species, breeding distribution and timing are related to sea-surface temperature.

THE LONG TERM

According to chief researcher Heike Lotze, humans have altered the Quoddy region ecosystem through "top down" impacts such as excessive fishing, hunting and harvesting. The result has been a decline in size and abundance of target species, shifts in dominant species and therefore shifts in food web structure.

Humans have also altered species composition and productivity through "bottom-up" impacts such as nutrient enrichment and shifts in nutrient ratios. These changes have altered species composition in the phytoplankton community and increased the occurrence and abundance of less edible and toxic species. Long-lived rockweeds and eelgrasses have declined, while annual algae blooms have increased.

Humans have altered the Quoddy ecosystem through "side-in" impacts such as habitat degradation and destruction, chemical contamination and physical disturbance. The extent of high quality spawning, breeding, nursing, feeding and staging grounds has declined, and multiple pollutants may have affected the health, survival and reproduction of species. Increasing human activities in and around coastal waters create stress and disturbance for birds, mammals and other species.

There are some encouraging trends, however. Laws protecting migratory birds and marine mammals and the establishment of sanctuaries have helped some populations move towards recovery over the past 70 years or so. Others, such as whales, continue to struggle. River pollution has improved and species such as gaspereau have demonstrated they will return if the physical conditions are right. Technical innovations such as 'pingers' attached to gillnets are reducing the incidence of harbor porpoise entanglements and deaths, and marine mammal recovery programs are releasing porpoises and whales unharmed from herring weirs. In other marine environments, such as the Baltic Sea, it is clear that measures to reduce nutrient loading have achieved dramatic improvements in habitat quality for marine species.

While parts of it seem to be in real trouble, the Quoddy region as a whole seems not to have lost its productive capacity as a marine ecosystem. If measures are taken to ensure species have adequate food, habitat and undisturbed space and time; to reduce the use of destructive and unselective fishing gear; to stop fishing down the food web; to protect those critical habitats used by many species at once and to reduce nutrient and toxic pollution, then this marine oasis can be sustained into the future.

No single measure is enough. The Conservation Council report makes it clear that multiple stresses over 200 years have collectively and synergistically resulted in troubling ecosystem and food web trends. Unless each of these stress points is dealt with through a combination of resource management changes, legislation and community action, it is very likely that the downward spiral will continue.

Janice Harvey is founder of the Conservation Council of New Brunswick. Photographs courtesy of the Charlotte County Historical Society, St. Andrews, New Brunswick

This article is based on a report describing the area within a line drawn from Point Lepreau on the north shore of the Bay of Fundy, south to the Grand Manan archipelago and west to the Maine shore, as a marine oasis of international significance. Authored by Dr. Heike Lotze of Dalhousie University and CCNB President Inka Milewski, *Two Hundred Years of the report*, describes the confluence of oceanographic, physical and biological features of the region which create its richness. It also describes some disturbing long-term trends which suggest its future may not be as rich as its past.

The full report, (165 pp.), is available from the Conservation Council of New Brunswick, 180 St. John Street, Fredericton, NB E3B 4A9, or by e-mail: ccnb@nb.aibn.com.

Maps for the Future

On a very local level, GIS technology offers great promise

CHRIS BREHME &
NATHAN MICHAUD

Maine has a long tradition of local control. Unfortunately, as its economy becomes less dependent on small-scale natural re-source production and more on the rapid movement of information, the state's smallest towns increasingly find themselves without the economic leverage they've had in the past. Add the elements of "sprawl"—most impor-tantly, the migration of young people out of rural towns and the movement of service-center commuters into them—and you have a precari-ous situation: small towns must make critical decisions about land-use policy, but they are in a poor position to do so because they lack the information they need. Migrations, moreover, can dilute the networks of relationships that give small towns their very identity, and they can create tensions between citizens who regard land in different ways.

Legend

First graders
- Ally
- Caitlin
- Marley
- Stephanie

Kindergarteners
- Ben
- Camille
- Dustin
- Jacob

Town Places
- Ferry
- Library
- School
- Town Offices

Stores
- Dark Harbor Shop
- Durkees
- Island Market

N

1 0 1 2 Miles

Map created by Ally Craig, Caitlin Small, Marley Babb, Stephanie Bethune, and Hannah Kerr
January 14, 2002

Kathy Hayes

Katleen Reardon with High School Junior Hannah Kerr. Facing page: An example of student work from Islesboro.

Often, problems create new opportunities. Geographic Information System (GIS) technology is becoming the common medium for the exchange and management of data about our physical world. In GIS, extensive databases are linked to maps which can allow you to display any combination of information "layers" in a map, and also to query the databases and represent the results visually. For example, a planning board looking to increase a buffer around a certain wetland from 75 to 100 feet could assess the impact of the proposed change visually, by displaying it on a computerized map. The board could then query the computer to produce a list of property owners affected by the change, another list of structures that would become non-conforming, and so on.

While this technology and the capacity to use it is still relatively rare among Maine towns, interest in GIS is increasing. Among Maine's islands, some of the smallest of the state's communities, at least three—Islesboro, Vinalhaven and Peaks—have invested in the creation of local GIS databases and are pursuing strategies for local empowerment through use of the technology locally. When well integrated into the community, GIS can help correct the urban-rural imbalance of information management capacity; it's possible to envision, as residents of these three islands have, GIS as the centerpiece of a sort of local "information commons," the maintenance and updating of which could truly be a community-wide process.

With a grant from the National Science Foundation, the community of Islesboro and the Island Institute are taking the first steps toward a community-integrated GIS. The end result will include a database of human and environmental features on the island, which can be described as a "community atlas." Beyond the data itself, the Islesboro GIS project seeks to become a catalyst for cooperation among the town, the school and the local land trust. These institutions have a history of working together on the island, and this project is designed to build on that foundation.

The project has assisted the community in purchasing GIS hardware and software, and provided a full-time Island Fellow to help coordinate the project. With a background in environmental and marine science, Kathleen Reardon has helped link GIS with applied science in the classroom and beyond. She taught a semester-long GIS science course to Islesboro high school students, who designed their own projects on the island. These projects reached out to other parts of the community, such as the groundwater protection committee, and demonstrated the utility of GIS for a variety of applications. Subsequently, Reardon decided to offer the GIS course through the local adult education program.

Reardon has also assisted several municipal committees in using GIS to manage and analyze their data. She has also worked with the local land trust to map new trails and scan and register aerial photographs. Alone, these tasks have helped community members save time and view their own information in new and interesting ways. Together, they represent an opportunity for the community of Islesboro to develop a model for the future.

By aggregating the information from various community institutions into a community atlas, Islesboro can create an image of the island that is the collective vision of the people who live there.

Quite independently, a structure similar to that on Islesboro is taking form on Vinalhaven, under the auspices of its ongoing comprehensive planning process. The Vinalhaven Land Trust, which was also extensively involved in the natural resources inventory for Vinalhaven's 1988 comprehensive plan, contracted with GIS specialists at College of the Atlantic in Bar Harbor to create one of the most thorough local GIS databases in the state. In anticipation of pursuing collaborative place-based education projects, the Vinalhaven school has also acquired GIS software. The GIS maps, which were received with much interest at a public meeting in January, will be a valuable planning tool as a means of tracking growth trends and may be used to create visualizations of "build-out" scenarios (i.e. what the island would look like if developed to the extent that current zoning allows). While the basic GIS data was compiled by COA, comprehensive planning committee members are also using the maps as a repository for information collected for the plan—for example, a database of various land uses is being tied to the digital parcel map, so that the use code (commercial/retail, residential/marine, etc.) of any parcel is a click away. The Land Trust and Comprehensive Planning Committees hope to create the capacity locally to continually update the system.

Island Institute Fellow James Essex was placed on Peaks Island in the fall of 2000 to create a GIS database there. Essex worked closely with Portland officials and Art Astarita of Peaks Island Land Preserve to build an accurate map set and database, which included tide lines, roads, walking trails, building footprints, parcel ownership data, water and sewer lines, shoreland topography and zoning. Peaks community members recently began a neighborhood planning process in coordination with Portland's comprehensive planning, and the GIS is sure to prove valuable. There is also interest within the community in using GIS as part of a more broadly-conceived Peaks Island Documentation Project, which, according to Peaks Island Neighborhood Association President Bill Hall, will be a "time capsule" of Peaks at the turn of the 21st century.

As each of these island communities is aware, however, new technologies also create new controversies. While what goes into GIS databases is almost always public information, the new format nonetheless brings to the fore questions of privacy, ownership and access. Some larger towns using GIS make the maps and data available through a website, while many small towns are understandably nervous about providing the world with quick and easy access to information about sensitive habitat, local hiking trails or property values. Indeed, to explore the use of GIS on a municipal level is to enter a conversation about information ownership and access, in which there aren't yet many ready answers. Nonetheless, by taking the initiative to explore the possibilities of new technology on a local level, these three island communities can ensure that the small town perspective has a place in this conversation.

Chris Brehme is GIS-website Director at the Island Institute. Nathan Michaud is the Institute's Community Planning Officer.

Looking

To Gretchen Dow Simpson,

Beyond

architecture is a surrogate

the

for the human presence

Obvious

CARL LITTLE

T he painter Gretchen Dow Simpson was born in Cambridge, Massachusetts, in 1939. She first came to Maine on a trip to Prout's Neck when she was 12 and a friend of her parents drove her to visit his daughter. "I remember him driving 100 miles an hour on the highway and showing me the speedometer," she recalls. "I thought, 'Wow, Maine is a wild place!' "

Simpson's introduction to island life happened four years later when she babysat for the Byrd family's four boys on Vinalhaven. She thought the island was the most beautiful place she had ever seen. She recalls the view looking across to North Haven, the clear air, the trees and, above all, the feeling of freedom.

Simpson attended Rhode Island School of Design in 1957–1959. She majored in painting, but after she left RISD she didn't take up a brush again until 1970. She worked at the 1964 World's Fair in New York; she learned how to type and took secretarial jobs in Boston. She started taking photographs of the buildings and set up a dark room in her kitchen. Eventually, she landed a job at an advertising agency in New York, starting as a secretary, but then becoming assistant to the photographer.

About 1970 Simpson started submitting work to *The New Yorker*. She describes these early pieces as "very rough, magic marker sketches, flowers on buildings and the like" She was also creating larger-than-life papier-mâché jewelry, some of which ended up featured in *Vogue*.

Left: *Maine II*, oil/linen, 30"x30", 2001

June 14, 1976   Price 75 cents

THE
NEW YORKER

The New Yorker responded favorably to the sketches and encouraged Simpson to keep sending art, which she did for nine years until a new art director, Lee Lorenz, took over. By that time she had started doing abstract paintings, which was what Lorenz liked. He suggested that she do realistic paintings with the feeling of abstract ones.

Not knowing what to paint, Simpson followed Lorenz's advice, which has stuck with her to this day: "Paint what you like to look at." She went to a friend's apartment, took some photographs of her hallway and made a painting. Lorenz bought the picture for *The New Yorker* in March 1974, "probably the most exciting day of my life," recounts Simpson, "besides giving birth to my daughters!" She has been using the camera to respond to the world ever since.

When she started doing cover art for *The New Yorker*, architecture provided a basis for form. Despite her interest in houses, she never considered becoming an architect—"too many rulers" is her simple explanation. In 1988, she adjusted her style and subject matter in response to the magazine's new editor, Robert Gottlieb, who wanted more punch and drama in his covers. Architectural studies in acrylic were replaced by cropped images of pumpkins, the American flag, rowboats and other objects executed in oils. "It was a progressive and wonderful learning experience for me," Simpson once said.

From 1978 to 1988 Simpson regularly visited her stepmother's house on Islesboro. Her list of special Maine pleasures includes many tied to the island: plunging into the cold water off the dock, kayaking, playing tennis surrounded by spruce trees, walking on the beach at low tide. She also has a great fondness for

Vinalhaven, acrylic/paper, 12"x16", 1993

Monhegan, recalling picnics on the rocks and hiking. Ferry rides to islands are, she says, "always an adventure."

The Islesboro Historical Society mounted an exhibition of Simpson's work in 1993; she remembers it as successful and fun. *Maine Times* art critic Edgar Allen Beem noted that seven of the 40 images in the exhibition "involve Maine subjects"— enough, as it were, to claim the painter as one of our own.

Beem drew a comparison between Simpson's work and that of Edward Hopper, how both use architecture "as a surrogate for the human presence." More than that, the painters share a fascination with architectural configurations, how one roofline plays off against another, how

windows lend a structure personality. And they recognize, in their own ways, how elements of a facade are receptacles of light and shadow that change in character, even in form, as the sun moves up or down the sky.

Among Simpson's favorite artists are two Italians, Piero della Francesca, the 15th-century master, and Georgio de Chirico, the great 20th-century metaphysical painter. The former's signature geometric perspective and the latter's sense of enigma find echoes in her studies of shadowed edifices and empty plazas. She has also felt a kinship with Charles Sheeler, Richard Diebenkorn, Rene Magritte and Man Ray—"and dancers of all kinds," she adds.

In her painting *Vinalhaven*, which shows the stairwell of the Washington School (now the home of the Vinalhaven Press), one recalls some of Hopper's later canvases, where he left out the figure and focused on the angles of an interior. Simpson seems less concerned with the psychological resonance of an empty space and more interested in the beauty of interlocking elements, the diagonal of a banister, the even strips of flooring and paneling.

On islands Simpson is drawn to the seeming simplicity of life, which she finds reflected in the architecture. She has painted several studies of structures on Islesboro, attracted to the geometric purity of outbuildings, a steep set of stairs, white clapboards, a red roof. She brings out the abstract quality of her subject matter, framing the scene before her in a photographic manner. Indeed, the camera continues to play a key role in her art. And the actual process of painting relates to photography: she works from faint to distinct, building the paint layer by layer, so that the image emerges like a photograph from the developer.

From time to time, Simpson turns to the landscape, choosing simple yet striking island motifs such as the silhouette of a spruce tree at sunset. *Islesboro #V* shows a rocky point of land reflected in the kind of still water Fitz Hugh Lane preferred. One has the sense one is at the end of some

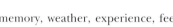

Gretchen Dow Simpson in Italy.

world, the island tapering off to ledges before a blank sky.

Of the more than 65 paintings that were used as covers by *The New Yorker* over a 20-year period, two were inspired by Maine islands. One is from Islesboro (a yellow house), the other, an image of rowboats on Monhegan, dating from the 1980s. She returned to the latter island this past year, photographed the same boats and did some "mature" paintings of them.

Simpson's art has always been related to place. Subject matter is often tied to

memory, weather, experience, feeling. In addition to Maine, she has painted Massachusetts, Block Island, Upper New York State, Morocco, Mexico, Italy, Cuba, Nova Scotia, New Hampshire and Providence, Rhode Island, where she lives.

All the while, Simpson has kept her Maine island connections, and they have left a lasting impression on her and her work. She loves having water in the distance, although she points out that her island paintings don't always have this element in them. "Just knowing that water is nearby is intriguing," she states. At the same time, she enjoys the isolation and sense of freedom, even though at times she can feel claustrophobic, which has been a surprise to her. She believes that that kind of contrast is the key to island existence.

Simpson has sought signs of what she terms a "primitive past" on Maine islands, and while she has been dismayed with the over development of these special places, she continues to find the simplicity that inspires her, like a backyard clothesline on Monhegan. "I'm not interested in making a political or environmental statement about the world," she once told a critic, "but I am very optimistic about preserving what's beautiful and in making people aware of looking beyond the obvious."

Monhegan Island II, oil/linen, 30"x30", 2000

Carl Little's most recent book is The Watercolors of John Singer Sargent *(University of California Press). He is Director of Communications at the Maine Community Foundation. New Yorker covers reprinted by permission; Copyright ©1976 (pg. 92) and ©1989 (pg. 91)* The New Yorker Magazine, Inc. *All rights reserved.*

"It's a pretty tough thing for a captain to do," says Cockburn, in an aside, "to hand over command of his ship to someone who he's only known for half an hour. This guy seems to be taking it pretty well."

LOCAL Knowledge

Continued from page 25

ing signals from other ships in similar need. And history is filled with the sorry stories of ships that were ignored by pilots, and ended up in pieces on the rocks. Ultimately, pilots organized to parcel out the work. By the 20th century, piloting was a more polite and professional business, although it remained rough work.

Aboard IZ, it's time to get down to business.

"Okay, Captain, I think we can get underway," says Cockburn. "Let's go dead slow ahead, please, rudder midships." The captain translates the orders into Croation, and a buzzer sounds, loudly. "Steady as she goes," adds Cockburn.

"It's a pretty tough thing for a captain to do," says Cockburn, in an aside, "to hand over command of his ship to someone who he's only known for half an hour. This guy seems to be taking it pretty well." And the trust has to go both ways, Cockburn says. It's his job to get this aging

vessel, brimming with millions of gallons of diesel fuel, up the river and into a tight docking space. To do that, he needs a ship that'll do what it's supposed to do. Cockburn has been given a spec sheet delineating the ship's particulars, its horsepower, how its steering works, what quantity of RPMs will get him what speed. But he's taking his time in the approach to the river in order to get a feel for how the ship handles. "It's kind of a strange relationship between the master of the vessel and

the pilot, where, you know, I'm depending on him to give me a good ship, and he's depending on me to do the right thing with it. So it's a tough thing, two people who haven't met and have to have that sort of trust."

Piloting a ship isn't like driving a car, says Cockburn. "In fact, it's just the opposite. When you turn a ship, the stern moves, so you have to be sort of aware of that, all the motion really is behind you, that's where the rudder is. And you just

The crew of the IZ

Tugs begin to position the ship into the berth at Sprague Energy in Bucksport.

push the tanker into the precise position to go under the bridge. It's a crucial moment; at its original draft, this ship only had about two or three feet of clearance under the span. At Cockburn's request, the captain has weighted down the stern with additional ballast, raising the bow and increasing that clearance by a few more feet.

Cockburn is busy now ordering the tugs to move a little bit ahead, asking the captain to stop the engine. It's a tight squeeze, but the IZ makes it with a few feet to spare. Earlier in the trip, there was a fair amount of informal chit-chat on the bridge, in both Croation and English. Now, the river has narrowed down considerably, and the channel, while deep, wiggles from right to left. Chit-chat has ceased, and everyone's concentrating. Throughout the morning, Cockburn has kept an intense eye on his computer screen, the ship's radar, and physical phenomena outside like the set of a buoy, the tops of trees, the trail that current leaves as it parts around an obstruction in the water.

"Hard to starboard, hard to starboard," he says, correcting the ship's course. Finally, about three and a half hours after leaving the Searsport Anchorage, the IZ nears its Bucksport berth. For almost an hour, Cockburn gives directions to the captain of the IZ, and the two tugboat captains as well. The ship is pulled forward and back, starboard and port. It vibrates as its engines reverse. Cockburn moves outside to give orders, so he can get a better view of the dock. He's in constant communication with the tugs, as the captain stands anxiously near him. "Up a notch on the VERONA, make it a half please," says Cockburn, and the tug toots in confirmation. At 12:15 lines are thrown, and the ship is finally secured. "Looks like we're in position, Jeff," says one of the tug captains. "How sweet was that?" asks Cockburn with a smile. Nobody ever parked their Toyota more elegantly.

Before it's time to leave, the man the Croatians call "Meester Pilot" is given a bottle of traditional Croation liquor—35 percent alcohol—by a grateful captain and Cockburn helps the captain with some unfinished business: "Match any of your numbers to the winning number," says Cockburn, as he and the captain hunch over the lottery ticket. "Here, start scratching like crazy." Cockburn heads home.

have to anticipate, this thing is not going to stop right now, so you have to have the speed under control."

Bucksport is 12 miles upriver from the Searsport anchorage. Cockburn takes on two tugs just off Fort Point, before he gets into what he calls the "meat of the river." Under Cockburn's direction, they'll eventually help maneuver the ship under the Waldo-Hancock bridge at Verona and into the berth at Sprague Energy in Bucksport.

Equally important to getting up this river are the electronic devices Cockburn uses. He arrived this morning with $10,000 worth of portable computers and software in his backpack. The first thing he did was set up his laptop on the bridge, and place an antenna outside to receive satellite signals. They tell him a variety of things: the ship's speed, the distance to the next navigation waypoint, whether the ship is to the right or left of the center of the course line, the time the ship is due to arrive and the condition of the satellites. The information his electronics give him about distances is accurate to within one foot. As the tugs, the MACK POINT and VERONA, toot in the background in response to Cockburn's radioed orders, they help

Naomi Schalit is a reporter with Maine Public Radio.

ISLAND INSTITUTE

Sustaining the Islands and Communities of the Gulf of Maine

Island life depends on community. Since 1983 the Island Institute's mission has been to provide programs and services that help sustain the islands and communities in the Gulf of Maine, comprised of people who depend on each other and on the resources of the sea.

The Institute's programs reflect the delicate balance between man and Nature, blending biology and sociology with today's technology. Island life is all about collaboration—between those who earn their living with a boat and a buoy, and those who may be guided by a computer or a satellite. The Island Institute is the oldest, strongest and most enduring advocate for ensuring the preservation of Maine's most endangered species—the island way of life.

FELLOWS

This program is designed to provide support to island communities through the efforts of recent college graduates who want to serve in Maine's island and coastal communities while gaining valuable field experience. These one- to two-year placements offer graduate-level students an opportunity to gain community development skills while living on one of Maine's year-round islands. This program is a partnership of the Island Institute, the selected Fellows and the host communities where the Fellows reside. To date the program has placed 17 Fellows in 11 communities, where Fellows work with a variety of community organizations on projects related to environmental and marine science, education and other areas, all determined by the community. Fellows are also expected to ensure that the skills and projects they bring to their host community will continue after their departure.

Thirty-two percent of the Institute's FY 01-02 operating budget of $2.8 million is expected to come from annual membership dues and personal and corporate donations. Foundations and grants are responsible for 55 percent, and institutional programs including publications and retail sales from Archipelago comprise 13 percent.

The Institute's annual report, listing members and presenting financial details, is available upon request.

MEMBERSHIP

The Island Institute currently has more than 4,000 members. They live on islands; they live on the mainland; they live out of state and visit in the summer. All of them believe in helping to sustain Maine's islands and remote coastal communities. Join the Institute and support Maine's only nonprofit organization dedicated to preserving a way of life for generations yet to come.

EXAMPLES OF COMMUNITY PROJECTS:

- Assisting with islands' comprehensive planning

- Developing research protocol and conducting marine research in collaboration with fishermen and collaborating organizations

- Providing technical training to island students and adult learners

- Designing and implementing new curricula in island schools

- Researching and writing grant proposals to support new technology and equipment in schools and libraries

- Automating, expanding and developing programming for island library collections

- Designing and implementing a series of after-school and summer activities for island children

BOAT DONATIONS

Boating in Maine is as popular as shopping in Freeport or climbing Cadillac Mountain. But when it's time to stop boating or perhaps get a new boat, many people choose to donate their boat to the Island Institute. Large or small, sail or power, the Institute will find a new home for your boat, even if we can't use it in our programs. If you would be interested in making such a gift, or know of someone who is, please contact us.

PLANNED GIVING

Contributing to the Island Institute through planned giving can provide a significant tax break for the donor while at the same time sustaining the communities and environment of the Gulf of Maine. A gift may generate a better return as a charitable donation than as a highly appreciated asset in your portfolio. The Island Institute offers a variety of planned giving options suited to your needs.

ISLAND INSTITUTE

386 Main Street
Rockland, Maine USA 04841
phone (207) 594-9209
fax (207) 594-9314
email institute@islandinstitute.org
www.islandinstitute.org

"Islanders are like endangered species: the islands themselves are durable, it's the communities that get blown away in time."

— Philip Conkling